Geology
Crafts
for Kids

Editor: Deborah Morgenthal
Art Director: Dana Irwin
Production: Elaine Thompson and Dana Irwin
Illustrations: Gwen Diehn
Photography: Evan Bracken

Library of Congress Cataloging-in-Publication Data

Anderson, Alan H.
        Geology crafts for kids: 50 nifty projects to explore the marvels of planet earth / Alan
Anderson, Gwen Diehn & Terry Krautwurst.
        p. cm
"A Sterling/Lark book."
Includes index.
ISBN 0-8069-8156-3
1. Geology--Experiments--Juvenile literature. [1. Geology--Experiments. 2. Experiments.] I. Diehn,
Gwen, 1943- .
II. Krautwurst, Terry, 1946- . III. Title.
QE29.A59 1996
551.078--dc20   96-1553
                                                                     CIP
                                                                     AC

10 9 8 7 6 5 4 3 2 1

A Sterling/Lark Book

Published in 1996 by Sterling Publishing Co., Inc.
    387 Park Avenue South, New York, NY 10016

Created and produced by Altamont Press, Inc.
    50 College Street, Asheville, NC 28801

©1996 Alan Anderson, Gwen Diehn, and Terry Krautwurst

Distributed in Canada by Sterling Publishing,
    c/o Canadian Manda Group, One Atlantic Avenue, Suite 105,
    Toronto, Ontario,Canada M6K 3E7

Distributed in Great Britain and Europe by Cassell PLC,
    Wellington House, 125 Strand, London, England WC2R 0BB

Distributed in Australia by Capricorn Link (Australia) Pty Ltd.
    P.O. Box 6651, Baulkham Hills Business Centre, NSW, Australia 2153

Additional photo credits:

Richard Babb, page 119; Bob Cetera, for Mammoth Cave National Park, page 142; Herman Hemler, for Carlsbad Caverns, page
87; Dana Irwin, Giza Pyramids and Santorini, page 124; Bob Lea, pages, 34 and 119; Chris McLaughlin, page 86; NASA, pages
6, 7, 23

U.S. Geologic Survey (USGS)—Carrara, P., page 101; Fries, C., page 14; Hansen, W.R., pages 55, 70, 93; Hamilton, W.B., pages 34,
37, 58, 60, 65, 87, 100, and 101; Huber, N.K., page 36; Keith, A., page 70; Lohman, S.W., pages 53 and 62; McKee, E.D., pages 94,
100, and 102; Ross, C.P., page 66; Stacy, J.R., page 26; Swanson, D.A., page 31; Trimble, D.E., page 58; USGS, pages 15, 19, 27, 30;
Witkind, I. J., page 64

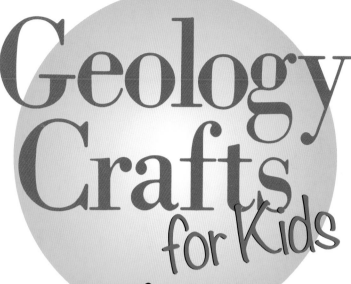

Geology Crafts
for Kids

50 Nifty Projects
to Explore the Marvels
of Planet Earth

Alan Anderson, Gwen Diehn
& Terry Krautwurst

Sterling Publishing Co., Inc.   New York
A STERLING/LARK BOOK

CONTENTS

= NEEDS ADULT HELP

introduction

*L*ike a volcano ready to erupt, this book is brimming with information about geology—written just for you. Each of the 34 sidebars are full of facts presented in a lively and exciting way. And to help you learn, there are 50 activities for you to do. You'll have hands-on fun as you learn about continental drift, earthquakes, crystals, erosion, map making, fossils—and yes—you even get to make a lava-spewing volcano!

For safety reasons, we strongly suggest you ask adults to help you with some of the projects. But please use good safety habits with all the activities. There is a drawback when adults help you with these projects: you may find they want to try everything in the book themselves! Discovering the marvels of Planet Earth captivates people of all ages.

The book is organized so that information builds from one chapter to the next. It's a good idea to start at the beginning and work your way to the end. However, if you can't help jumping right into something that interests you on page 95, that's fine; use the index to help you find an explanation of a topic or term you may have skipped.

Two more tips: Read the instructions all the way through once or even twice before you start. This will help you understand what you're about to do. And make sure you have all the materials you need before you begin a project. It's very frustrating to realize you can't finish the experiment because of a missing ingredient.

Peacock pyrite

The subject of geology is so broad and complex that there is always more to learn. If you get fascinated by one of the topics presented here, we hope you'll look for other books on that subject. So let's gear up and get started! There's a lot of *ground* to cover!

Chapter 1

All About the Earth

This planet of ours called Earth is a really amazing place. Here we are on a rocky, spinning ball that's whizzing through space at almost 45,000 miles (72,000 km) an hour. (Whoa! Hold on to your hat!) The eight other planets in our solar system are traveling that fast, too. But as far as anybody knows only Planet Earth is carrying the likes of cheeseburgers, skateboards, Godzilla movies, and about six billion two-legged creatures who like to call themselves "intelligent life."

Over the years, some of the most inquisitive creatures, known as scientists, have learned a lot about Earth and its place in the universe. For instance, we know that our solar system is just one of more than 100,000 million other solar systems in our galaxy. And there are at least 10,000 million other galaxies in the universe!

When you look at it that way, Earth seems awfully tiny. Even compared to the four largest planets in our own solar system, Earth is small. But here at ground level, Earth is more than big enough to give scientists and other curious people (like you) a lot to learn and discover.

After all, our planet's surface—its continents and oceans and mountains and valleys and deserts and all the rest—covers nearly 197 million square miles (512 million sq km). The Earth is 24,902 miles (39,843 km) around at the equator, and 24,859 miles (39,774 km) around at the poles. If you walked every day and every night without stopping to rest, it would take you more than a year to walk all the way around the globe!

Earth is so big that it fools our eyes. To a five-foot human, a mile-high mountain is huge. And look at the Grand Canyon! Now that's a big hole! So most people think that our planet is rough and bumpy. But for its size, Earth is actually surprisingly smooth. If you were to shrink it down to the size of a bowling ball, it would be even smoother than the real thing.

Here's another way Earth tricked our ancestors' eyes. For hundreds of years people thought that the Earth was flat because the world looks flat when you gaze at the horizon. Of course, these days we know better. The world is round, right? Umm, well, not exactly. Actually, because it's slightly bigger at the equator than at the poles, Earth isn't truly round. It bulges in the middle and flattens just a bit at the top and bottom. Scientists call anything with this particular shape a *geoid* ("earth-shaped").

A fantastic view of the sphere of the Earth as photographed from the Apollo 17 spacecraft during the final lunar landing mission in NASA's Apollo program

In this chapter, we're going to learn how old the Earth is, what it's made of, why its insides are so hot, how and why earthquakes happen, what causes mountains to rise, and much more. So fasten your seat belt and get ready to ride…to the tops of mountains…to the bottoms of oceans…and down deep inside the fiery core of Planet Earth!

How Old Is Earth? How Old Is That?

Scientists think that our planet is about 4.6 billion years old. Obviously, that's really, really old—but just how old?

To help you get a better idea of how long ago 4.6 billion years is, imagine that Earth is ten years old instead of 4.6 billion.

Ten years ago our newborn planet was just beginning to form an outer crust. It was mostly a big, molten ball of dust and gas left over when a much, much larger ball of dust and gas collapsed on itself and formed the hot, shining star we call the Sun. Back in those days there were a few other leftover balls circling the Sun, too. Some were smaller than Baby Earth, some larger. Some were closer to the Sun, some farther away. Today we call them the planets. Together they make up our Solar System.

You wouldn't have wanted to be anywhere near Earth during those first couple of toddler years. Talk about the Terrible Twos! There were no seas or land. You couldn't breathe the air. Virtually everything was hot and molten. Meteorites and asteroids and comets kept crashing into the red-hot planet.

Eventually, about **eight years ago**, things cooled down. Rocks began to form, creating a thicker crust. Water from steam collected on the surface, forming shallow seas. And the first signs of life—bacteria—appeared.

A little more than a billion years later—about **five of our imaginary years ago**—you were really hot stuff if you were pond scum. You and other members of the blue-green algae family were the most advanced forms of life on earth.

It wasn't until **last year** that the first plants on land showed up. Meanwhile, giant sea scorpions as much as nine feet long roamed the oceans.

About **eight months ago**, lush swamps of mosses and tall-as-trees ferns covered the land. Today, their fossils make up most of the world's coal beds.

Six months ago, the first dinosaurs appeared. **A month and a half ago**, they became extinct.

Our earliest ancestors, big-brained hairy creatures who could actually walk on two legs instead of four, showed up about a **day and a half ago**.

The first true humans, or animals who looked more or less like your Uncle Bill when he gets up in the morning, started tromping around in East Africa and Asia about **two hours ago**.

Eleven minutes ago the last Ice Age, when glaciers covered most of the Northern Hemisphere, finally ended.

Late afternoon over the Andes Mountains with sun glare, heavy cloud illumination, and sunlight against the Pacific Ocean

Thomas Jefferson signed the Declaration of Independence **15 seconds ago**.

Neil Armstrong, the first human on the moon, took a small step for man and a giant leap for mankind a little less than **two seconds ago**.

And you? How long have you been around?

Wink your eye once, fast. If you actually are ten years old, that's how long you've lived compared to the long, long, long life of Planet Earth.

GEOLOGIST'S Notebook

THIS BOOK IS MODELED AFTER AN OLD JAPANESE STYLE OF BOOK. IT MAKES AN EASY-TO-CARRY FIELD NOTEBOOK. DECORATE THE COVER WITH GRANITE PAPER (SEE PAGE 54) OR ANY OTHER FANCY PAPER.

- *Ruler*
- *Pencil*
- *Scissors*
- *12 to 15 sheets of white paper, 8½ by 11 inches (22 by 28 cm)*
- *Light, bendable cardboard such as poster paper or railroad board or tagboard for the cover, cut the same size as the page papers PLUS an extra ½ inch (1.5 cm) in width. The cover for the book shown here is 4½ by 11½ inches (11.5 by 29.5 cm).*
- *Paper clip*
- *Fancy paper to wrap the cover, sized slightly smaller than the cover itself. The granite paper on the cover of the book measures 4 by 9½ inches (10 by 24.5 cm).*
- *Large metal paper clamp*
- *Several pieces of scrap cardboard to use as a surface for hole poking*
- *Awl (sold at hardware stores)*
- *4 feet (1.2 m) of string or heavy thread*
- *Sewing needle with a large eye*
- *1 bead (optional; learn how to make one on page 82)*

W HAT YOU DO

1. Stack four or five sheets of paper neatly and fold them in half with a strong crease. Tear or cut the paper at the fold line. Repeat this with more paper until you have 21 pieces. Use the ruler and pencil to measure one piece of paper so that it is 4½ by 11 inches (11.5 by 28 cm). You can make the book any size, but keep in mind that the paper will be folded in half, so it must start out measuring twice as wide as the book pages will be.

2. Pick up six pieces of page paper at a time, stack them evenly, and fold them in half all at once. You will do this three times. You should now have three folded stacks of paper (called signatures) and three leftover sheets.

3. Place one of the signatures against one end of the outside of the cover cardboard with the folded end toward the middle of the cover. **1**

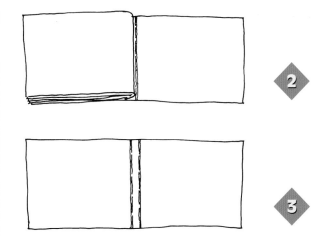

4. Use the rounded edge of the paper clip to press or score a line on the cover cardboard along the folded edge of the signature. Move the signature out of the way. Hold the ruler along the scored line and score this line hard several more times to make sure the line is straight. Scoring a line makes it fold more easily.

5. Place the signature against the other end of the cover **2**, and score a second line along the folded edge, just as you did before. Now your cover looks like figure **3**.

6. Lay the fancy paper, outside facing up, over the cover cardboard so that it is centered evenly. You should be able to see the ends of the scored lines above and below the fancy paper. **4** Lay the ruler

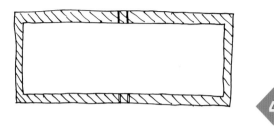

along the scored lines, over the fancy paper, and score the fancy paper along the scored lines in the cover. **5**

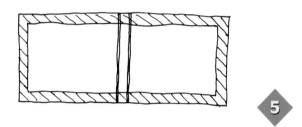

7. Carefully fold both the cover cardboard and the fancy paper together along the scored lines. Slip the three signatures inside the cover, pushing them firmly against the folded spine of the notebook. **6**

8. Trim 1 inch (2.5 cm) off the end of each of the three leftover pieces of paper, and slip these into the note-book at the back. They will stick out beyond the end of the book for now.

9. Clamp the entire book together with the large paper clamp so that nothing can move during the next part of the process.

10. **Ask an adult to help you with this step.** Use the awl to poke two holes about 1 inch (2.5 cm) down from the top and bottom edges, and ½ inch (1.5 cm) in from the spine of the notebook. You or an adult will have to screw the awl back and forth to make it go through all the thicknesses of paper. **7**

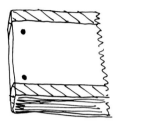

11. Turn the book over while it is still clamped and widen out the holes from the back.

12. Thread the needle. Stick the needle into either hole. Pull the thread until a tail 12 inches (30 cm) long is left. Hold that tail in place while you wrap the thread around the outside of the book and go back into the same hole. Pull tight.

13. Tie the two ends of thread together tightly on the spine of the notebook. **8**

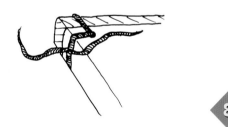

14. Repeat steps 12 and 13 for the other hole.

15. Cut the tails off evenly and either thread a bead through one thread (such as in the book shown here) or braid the tails, or fray them, or tie them together, or make bows, or cut them off short. Fold the three pages that are sticking out of the book in half so that their folded edges line up with the rest of the pages in the book. Use these extra long pages when you need a bigger sheet of paper.

PLANET *Mobile* ☉

THIS PAPIER-MÂCHÉ MOBILE SHOWS
YOU EARTH'S SIZE COMPARED TO
THE OTHER PLANETS IN OUR SOLAR
SYSTEM, AS WELL AS THE RELATIVE
DISTANCE OF ALL THE PLANETS FROM
THE SUN. IF YOU HANG THE MOBILE
IN A SUNNY WINDOW, YOU CAN WATCH
THE REAL SUN LIGHT UP ONE SIDE OF
EACH PLANET, LEAVING THE OTHER
SIDE IN DARKNESS, JUST LIKE DAY
AND NIGHT ON EARTH.

WHAT YOU NEED

- *Old broomstick, mop handle, or 1-inch-wide (2.54 cm) dowel, at least 42 inches (107 cm) long*
- *Old newspapers*
- *Spool of heavy thread or container of waxed dental floss*
- *Scissors*
- *Package of aluminum foil*
- *1 green pea*
- *8 paper clips*
- *1 small lime*
- *1 marble*
- *1 large cabbage*
- *1 orange*
- *1 grapefruit*
- *Water*
- *Mixing bowl or plastic dishpan*
- *2 cups (250 g) of all-purpose white flour*
- *Measuring cup*
- *Large cooking pot*
- *Spoon*
- *Acrylic paints*
- *Paintbrushes*
- *Old aluminum pie pan*
- *2 nails, ½-inch (1.3 cm) long*
- *Hammer*
- *Piece of colorful, sturdy yarn, 5 feet (1.5 m) long*

WHAT YOU DO

1. It helps to do this project if you first set up a convenient work space. Find two chairs that are the same height and move them about 3 feet (91 cm) apart, so that you can rest the broomstick, mop handle, or dowel across the backs of the chairs. Spread old newspapers on the floor under the broomstick.

2. First you must make an *armature* for each planet. An armature is an inside framework that keeps you from needing too much heavy, wet papier-mâché. You will make your armatures out of aluminum foil. Begin by cutting nine pieces of thread or dental floss, each at least 3 feet (91 cm) long. Tie a very fat knot (or several knots, one on top of the other) at the end of the first string. Now make a ball of aluminum foil around this knot. The ball should be the size of the green pea. You now have an armature for the planet Mercury hanging from the end of a thread. Eat the green pea and move onto the next planet.

3. For all the rest of the planets you will begin by tying a paper clip to the end of a piece of thread. You will then make a ball of aluminum foil around the paper clip. The size of the balls are as follows:

   Venus—a small lime

   Earth—a slightly bigger lime

   Mars—a marble

   Jupiter—a large, 9-inch (23 cm) cabbage

   Saturn—an 8-inch (20 cm) cabbage

   Uranus—an orange

   Neptune—a grapefruit

   Pluto—a marble

4. Tie the planets onto the broomstick like this: First make a mark 2 inches (5 cm) from the left end of the broomstick. Call this mark the sun. (Later you can paint that end of the broomstick yellow or orange.) Tie Mercury ½ inch (1.2 cm) away from the sun; Venus 1 inch (2.5 cm) from the sun; Earth 1½ inches

(4 cm) from the sun; Mars 2 inches (5 cm) from the sun; Jupiter 5 inches 12 cm) from the sun; Saturn 9½ inches (24 cm) from the sun; Uranus 19½ inches (50 cm) from the sun; Neptune 30 inches (75 cm) from the sun; and Pluto 39¾ inches (102 cm) from the sun.

5. Now it's time to make the papier-mâché. First you must tear three or four sections of old newspaper into strips about 1 inch (2.5 cm) wide and 3 inches (8 cm) long. Put these strips in warm water in the mixing bowl to soak for two hours while you take a break.

aluminum foil and to round and smooth out the surfaces of the planets. You should put the papier-mâché on in layers, and let it dry completely every time you have built up a layer of ⅛ inch (.5 cm) or so. You don't want it to get too thick or heavy or it will take too long to dry. It shouldn't take more than two layers to finish your planets. Many of the planets themselves have craters and mountains, so it's fine if your model planets do, too.

9. After the planets have dried completely, paint them. You can also paint the broomstick. Be sure to paint the left end of the broomstick up to the "sun" mark a bright yellow or orange to show where the sun is in relation to the planets. The colors of the planets that we can see with our bare eyes are as follows:

Mercury—lead gray

Venus—silver

Earth—blue and green

Mars—red

Jupiter—whitish yellow

Saturn—yellow

Uranus, **Neptune**, and **Pluto**—Because these planets can't be seen by earthlings using just our eyes, paint them gray or dull silver.

6. After your break, drain the water from the bowl of newspaper strips. Then mix 1 cup of flour (125 g) with 6 cups (1.5 l) of water in the cooking pot. **Ask an adult to help you put the pot onto the stove over moderate heat.** Stir the paste until it gets as thick as melted ice cream, then remove the pot from the heat and let it cool slightly.

7. Pour the lukewarm paste into the wet newspaper strips and mix thoroughly. You can mix with your hands or the spoon. It feels good to work with the warm paste, so don't cool the paste completely.

8. Now you will put strips and globs of papier-mâché all over your planets to completely cover the

10. Hammer a nail into each end of the broomstick or dowel. Tie the yarn to these two nails so that you can hang the mobile.

Molten to the Core

*N*o matter where you are right now, there are about 8,000 miles (12,800 km) of Planet Earth beneath your feet, and almost all of it is rock. True, water covers more than two-thirds of the globe's surface. But even the deepest parts of the oceans reach less than seven miles (11 km) to the sea floor. Compared to the thousands of miles of rock beneath them, our oceans don't amount to much more than a thin film of moisture—about as much as the morning dew on an apple! (That's why it's so important to take good care of the water we have.)

Scientists call the planet's water layer—our oceans, rivers, lakes, and streams—the *hydrosphere.* The air above, of course, is called the *atmosphere.*

The solid parts of our planet are made up of layers, too. When Earth was formed, gravity sorted out all the ingredients. The heaviest materials, such as iron, were pulled toward the center. Lighter elements stayed closer to the surface.

That's why Earth's *crust*—the planet's outer layer—is made up of fairly "light" rocks. The upper or *continental crust* forms the continents and is made of granite and other ancient rock that has been pushed and

— crust

ʌ\|\|\| upper mantle

lower mantle

outer core

● inner core

shoved and jumbled around a lot over the years. This part of the crust is as much as 60 miles (96 km) thick. The lower or *oceanic crust*, the part beneath the oceans, is much thinner, only about three miles (4.8 km), and is made of younger rock called *basalt.*

Earth's crust is the part we know the most about, because, after all, we live on it. Compared to the rest of the planet the crust is as thin as the skin on that apple we mentioned. And it's comfortably cool, too—unlike Earth's sizzling inside layers.

Below the crust is a layer of hot, heavy rock about 1,800 miles (2,880 km) thick. Scientists call this layer the *mantle.* Together, the crust and the upper part of the mantle are called the *lithosphere.* It's really toasty down there—between 1,600 and 5,500°F (870 to 3,035°C)! It's so hot, in fact, that in places the mantle rock isn't quite solid. It's thick and flexible—like Silly Putty™. Scientists think that some of these parts ooze in currents, like gummy rivers.

Beneath the mantle is an even heavier, hotter layer called the *outer core.* It's made mostly of the metals iron and nickel—liquid iron and nickel, that is. The entire outer core is melted through and through, and no wonder. The temperature is a scorching 5,500 to 7,200°F (3,035 to 3,978°C)!

Finally, at the very center of Earth is the *inner core,* a ball of solid iron nearly 800 miles (1,280 km) thick from its outside to its middle. Whew! Somebody open a window! The coolest part of the core is about 6,000°F (3,312°C), and the hottest part is nearly 12,000°F (6,642°C)—that's hotter than the surface of the sun!

But wait a minute. If Earth's inner core is so hot, how come it's solid instead of molten, like the outer core? Because so much weight is pushing in on the core from all directions, its molecules don't have any room to move apart. They stay packed together—solid as a rock.

Pot holes eroded in columnar basalt

Why Are Earth's Insides So Hot?

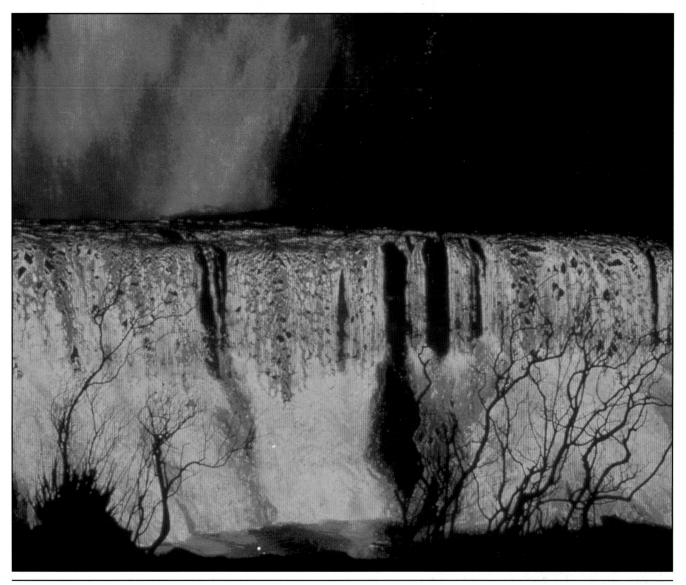

Eruption of Mount Kilauea. Hawaii National Park, 1969

You don't have to look much further than the steaming lava erupting from a volcano to know that Earth's insides are hot—super hot. But why? What makes all that heat? Is there a fire down there somewhere?

Scientists think most of inner Earth's heat was trapped billions of years ago, when the planet was being formed from chunks of space matter. Because of gravity, materials piling up on the outside squeezed materials inside. The squeezing generated heat. Plus, the searing-hot meteors and asteroids that were crashing into earth stayed hot as their pieces were pushed deeper into the planet.

The pressure from Earth's outer layers pushing inward still produces a lot of heat. And as radioactive materials inside the Earth decay, they give off even more heat.

In a way, then, there is a fire down there—a fire that's been burning for more than three billion years!

EARTH *Balls*

Here's a geological model that's fun to build, lets you see what the inside of the earth looks like, and is delicious as well as nutritious to eat! If people tell you to stop playing with your food, explain that you're actually learning geology, and then invite them to join you for a snack of yummy earth balls.

WHAT YOU NEED

For 6 to 8 earth balls:
- *Large bowl*
- *Spoon*
- *Measuring cups*
- *¼ cup (31 g) of powdered milk (noninstant is best, but instant will do)*
- *½ cup (170 g) of creamy peanut butter*
- *¼ cup (100 g) of honey*
- *Waxed paper*
- *Dull dinner knife*
- *½ cup (170 g) of strawberry, cherry, or raspberry jam*
- *½ cup (110 g) of chocolate chips*
- *½ cup (70 g) of sesame seeds or graham cracker crumbs*

1. Wash your hands.

2. Put ½ cup (170 g) of peanut butter and ¼ cup (31 g) of powdered milk into the bowl. Mix it with the spoon or with your hands. Add 1 teaspoon of honey in order to make a stiff dough. You may need more (or less) honey depending on how stiff or runny the peanut butter is. Keep adding honey a little at a time until the dough feels like clay dough.

3. Scoop up a small, round spoonful of dough and roll it into a ball.

4. Put the ball down on a piece of waxed paper and carefully cut the ball in half. Be careful not to squash the ball when you cut it.

5. Use the tip of the spoon handle to scoop out a small hole in the center of each half of the ball. The hole should be about the size of the tip of your little finger.

6. Use the spoon handle tip to put a small amount of jam into the holes you have scooped out. Now place a single chocolate chip in the middle of the jam in one of the halves of the ball. Don't put a chocolate chip in the other half. You now have created the core of the earth (the chocolate chip), surrounded by the hot, molten outer core (the jam)—all surrounded by the semiliquid magma (peanut butter mixture)!

7. Place the two halves of the ball back together and roll it a little in your hands to seal the seam.

8. Pour out about ½ cup (70 g) of sesame seeds or graham cracker crumbs onto another piece of waxed paper. Roll the ball around in the seeds or crumbs to thoroughly coat it. This coating is the rocky crust of the earth.

9. To complete the experiment, carefully cut the ball in half again so that you can see the layers: core, outer core, magma, and crust. Think about the real earth and its layers as you slowly chew your earth ball. Earth balls are so delicious that you'll want to make more to snack on and give to friends. Stored in the refrigerator in a closed container, they will keep for a long time.

Our Ever-Moving, Ever-Changing World

Try this: Go outside and jump up and down a couple of times. Did you feel the Earth shake? Now try this: Stand very, very still. Did you feel the ground moving? Of course not. We humans aren't sensitive enough to notice. But the ground beneath your feet actually is (s-l-o-w-l-y) moving all the time. Every once in a while it moves too noticeably—in an earthquake, for instance.

Solid as it seems, Earth's crust is a not-quite-connected crazy quilt of huge pieces, or *plates*, dozens of miles thick, restlessly pushing and shoving and bumping and scraping and pulling apart and jamming together. Each plate is attached to a piece of Earth's upper mantle, and together they ride on top of the partly molten, putty-like layer in the mantle called the *asthenosphere* (az-THEN-uh-sfeer).

Heat from Earth's core and lower mantle causes currents of oozing rock in the asthenosphere. These currents, called *convection cells*, slowly rise and fall, moving the plates above. (Check out the experiments on pages 20 to 22 for a firsthand look at the ups and downs of convection cells.) The study of how the pieces of Earth's crust move is called *plate tectonics* (tek-TAHN-iks).

Most of the action in Earth's crust happens at the seams, or cracks, where plates meet. In the Pacific Ocean, at least five large plates come together. That's why there are so many volcanoes and earthquakes in China, Japan, Hawaii, and California. There are a lot of places where chunks of the Earth are grinding together or moving apart.

Geologists think that different types of plate seams cause different kinds of Earth-changing actions. One happens in the oceans, along underwater ridges that stretch for thousands of miles. In these places, the Earth constantly grows new crust. Molten rock from the mantle oozes up through the crack between plates and into the sea water, where it cools and hardens and becomes part of the plates on either side. Convection currents in the mantle drive the plates apart. Then, new, hot material rises into the widening crack. **1**

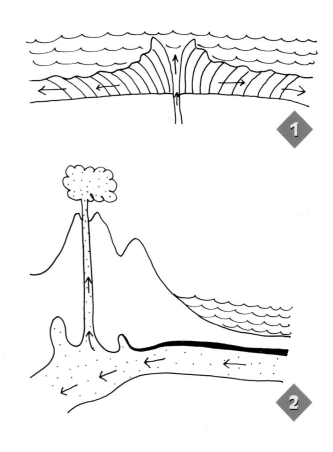

Meanwhile, in other places, the edges of ocean plates (which are made of heavy rock) are pushed under continental plates (which are lighter). The old ocean crust is shoved back down into Earth's mantle, where it melts as it sinks deeper into the planet's insides. Eventually, the hot, gooey rock will rise back up in a convection cell at an oceanic ridge and become part of Earth's crust again. Or it might find its way to a "hot spot," where it can gush upward through a long, deep opening and erupt on the surface. We call those places volcanoes. **2**

When plates push against one another, something's got to give. If they collide head-on, the edges of both plates slowly buckle upward, forming mountains. That's how the Alps and the Himalayas came to be. Not all plates push straight into each other, though. The plates along California's famous San Andreas Fault grind against each other sideways. Most of the time, neither side moves

**Rockslide
avalanche
on Sherman
Glacier,
caused by
Alaska earth-
quake, 1964**

much. The plates stay pressed together. Every once in a while, though, the plates slip apart—and then lock together again. Usually the plates slip just a little, not even enough for a person to notice. But sometimes the plates jerk apart with a lurch, making the ground shake or, when the plates slip a lot, causing earthquakes and landslides.

This sort of push and pull is happening all the time, in places all over the world where plates of Earth's crust meet. Our planet is constantly recycling its rock and reshaping its surface.

MOVING *Liquid*

A MODEL CONVECTION CELL

To try to understand pressure changes and movement in the earth's crust, geologists study what is called the *convection current theory*. The difference in temperature between the extremely hot center or core of the earth and the cooler mantle (molten rock) causes slow movement of the rocks that form the earth's crust.

Here's how geologists think that works: Hot molecules dance around faster than cool ones do. This fast movement causes the molecules to spread farther apart and to be less densely packed than cooler molecules. When a liquid is heated, it is, therefore, lighter and less dense than when it is cool. We know that lighter, less dense objects tend to float on top of denser, heavier substances. The hot core of the earth is constantly heating up the mantle that is closest to it. This hot liquid rock, being less dense and therefore lighter, rises very slowly toward the crust, or surface, of the earth. As it rises it cools and becomes heavier, and therefore sinks back down. This rising and sinking forms what scientists call giant convection cells in the earth's mantle. The plates of the earth's crust, riding on the mantle, move along very slowly on the convection cells—a few inches a year at most—like giant rafts floating on very slowly moving water.

The following two experiments will let you see how heat can move a liquid. Keep in mind that liquid rock moves much more slowly than water does, but the process is the same.

Experiment #1

WHAT YOU NEED

- *Large clear glass container, such as a glass mixing bowl, at least 7 inches (18 cm) tall*
- *Container of cold water*
- *Small glass jar, no more than 2 or 3 inches (5 or 8 cm) tall*
- *Handful of marbles or clean pebbles*
- *Container of very hot water*
- *Food coloring*
- *Piece of aluminum foil 4 by 4 inches (10 by 10 cm)*
- *Rubber band*
- *Towel*
- *Notebook*
- *Pencil*

WHAT YOU DO

1. Fill the large bowl with cold water, at least 6 inches (15 cm) deep. A good plan is to fill it and then put it in a refrigerator or freezer for a few minutes while you're getting the jar ready.

2. Put a layer of marbles or pebbles in the bottom of the jar to weight it. Fill the jar with very hot water. Try filling it with hot tap water and then sitting it in a pan of even hotter water for a few minutes. Ask an adult to help you prepare and pour the very hot water.

3. Add several drops of food coloring to the water in the jar. Tear a small hole, about the size of your thumbnail, in the center of the piece of aluminum foil. Cover the jar with the aluminum foil, centering the hole. Press the foil to fit the jar opening, and then hold it in place with the rubber band. What you are doing is making a smaller opening for the hot water to come out of.

4. Remove the bowl of cold water from the refrigerator. Holding the jar right side up and with your thumb over the hole, quickly place the jar on the bottom of the bowl, under the level of the cold water. You'll probably see and hear a few bubbles as air rushes out of the jar.

5. Now watch what happens. You can tell where the hot water is because it is colored. Use the towel to wipe the beads of moisture from the outside of the bowl in order to have a clear view of what's happening.

6. If the jar represents the hot core of the earth, what happens to the liquid rock that has been heated up by it? Where does this "hot rock" go? What happens after that "hot rock" cools down? Watch the surface of the water for currents. Is the water in motion? What's causing the motion in your model convection cell? Make notes in your notebook about this experiment.

Experiment #2

THIS EXPERIMENT SHOWS HOW HEAT MOVES WATER AND ALSO HOW A MATERIAL FLOATING ON A MOVING LIQUID MOVES WITH IT. IMAGINE THAT THE WATER IS THE SLOWLY MOVING BOTTOM LAYER OF THE EARTH'S CRUST.

WHAT YOU NEED

- *2-quart (1.9 l) cooking pot, full of water*
- *Stove*
- *Some dried herbs, such as rosemary, basil, or oregano—or some dry sawdust*
- *Notebook*
- *Pencil*

WHAT YOU DO

1. **Ask an adult to help you with this experiment** because you will need to use a hot stove and boiling water. Place the pot half on and half off one of the burners. (You are trying to make one part of the pot hotter than the other.)

2. Turn on the stove burner to high. As the water begins to boil (you'll see tiny bubbles forming on the bottom of the pot), sprinkle a thin layer of dried herbs or sawdust on top of the water. Watch what happens. Think of the dry particles as the earth's crust plates riding on the liquid mantle of the earth.

3. Notice where the herbs or sawdust go. Where do the particles gather? Do they gather over the hotter or the cooler part of the pot? Why? What does the movement of the herbs or sawdust tell you about the movement of the water? How is this a model of a convection cell? The dry particles gather where the cooler current sinks and move away from the spot where the hotter water rises. Why does this happen? Make notes in your notebook about this experiment.

Pangaea, Laurasia, and Gondwana

Earth's plates have been moving around and pulling apart and bumping into each other for a long time. It's no wonder the world has gone through a lot of changes.

Take our continents, for instance. You may have looked at a globe or map of the world and thought, gosh, those continents look like puzzle pieces. If you moved them around, some of them would fit together. Look at South America and Africa—if you pushed them towards each other, they'd match up perfectly side by side! Maybe they were connected once, and then just sort of, er, you know, floated apart.

Floated apart? The continents? Millions of tons of rock? Get outta here! Until recently, that was pretty much how most scientists reacted when anyone suggested that maybe the continents had been connected long ago and then somehow moved apart. A German scientist, Alfred Wegener, was the first to study the idea and say that it might be true. He came up with some pretty convincing evidence, too. He discovered that the same types of rock, and fossils of the same kinds of creatures, could be found in places where the continental "puzzle pieces" fit, even though those places were separated by hundreds of miles of oceans.

But it wasn't until 20 years after Alfred Wegener's death that geologists realized he was right. The continents

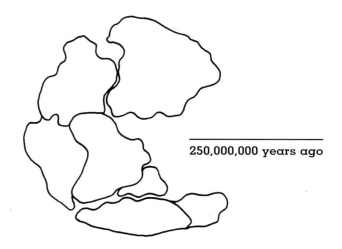

250,000,000 years ago

and ocean floors really do "float" on moving rock plates, and have been for millions of years.

They're floating right now. If you're ten years old, North America and Europe are about one foot farther apart today than they were on the day you were born. In some places the continents are moving about an inch (2.54 cm) a year. In other places, they're drifting as much as four inches (10 cm) a year.

Over time, continents drifting a few inches a year can make a b-i-g difference.

About 250 million years ago, all the continents on Earth were connected in a single land mass near the equator. Alfred Wegener called it *Pangaea* (Pan-GEE-uh), which means "all earth."

Around 200 million years ago, Pangaea split into two super-continents that gradually drifted apart. *Laurasia*, in the north, included the land that would become North America, Europe, and Asia. *Gondwana*, in the south, included South America, Africa, India, Antarctica, and Australia.

Over the next 100 million years, the land that was to become India drifted northward and eventually crashed into Asia, creating a huge pileup of rock we call the Himalayas. Australia broke away from what would be Antarctica. A split opened between South

Snow-dusted ranges on the Tibetan Plateau, showing the Vale of Kashmir in northern India, the major valley within the Himalaya Mountains

America and Africa, and also between North America and what would be Europe and Asia. The narrow strip of seawater in the middle was a baby ocean. It's a lot wider now. We call it the Atlantic.

With the help of computers, geologists are using their knowledge of how and where plates move to figure out what our world might look like in the future. Some predict that the Mediterranean Sea will disappear, that the Red Sea will become a new ocean, and that Australia will float to the equator. Don't hold your breath, though. These changes will take about 75 million years to happen!

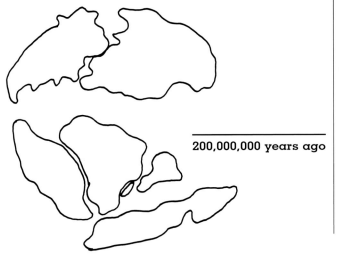

200,000,000 years ago

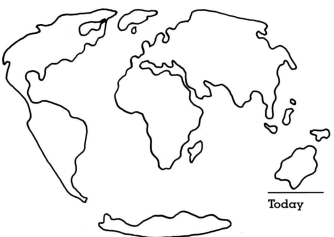

Today

JIGSAW *Puzzle*

IT'S FUN TO THINK OF THE ANCIENT CONTINENTS FITTING BACK TOGETHER LIKE GIANT JIGSAW PUZZLE PIECES. IT'S EVEN MORE FUN TO MAKE A MODEL OUT OF SALT DOUGH AND SEE FOR YOURSELF HOW THEY USED TO BE CONNECTED.

W**HAT YOU NEED**

- *Several sheets of tracing paper*
- *Pencil*
- *Scissors*
- *2 cups (250 g) of flour (plain white, unbleached, or bread flour work best)*
- *2 cups (192 g) of table salt*
- *2 tablespoons of dry wallpaper paste*
- *Spoon*
- *Large bowl*
- *2 cups (473.2 ml) of water*
- *Rolling pin*
- *Dull table knife*
- *Cookie sheet or pizza pan*
- *Oven*
- *Hot pad*
- *Acrylic paints*
- *Paintbrush*

WHAT YOU DO

1. Enlarge the pattern on a copier as indicated. Carefully trace it and cut out the pieces. Set them aside.

2. Mix the flour, salt, and wallpaper paste in the large bowl. Add 1 cup (236.6 ml) of water and mix, then slowly add as much of the rest of the water as you need to make a firm dough. The dough should not be runny, but should feel like stiff clay.

3. When the dough is sticking together but is still pretty crumbly, dump it out onto a floured countertop or table and knead it for about five minutes. Here is how to knead dough: Starting with a mound of dough, squeeze it and push it away from you at the same time, then pull it toward you, folding the top toward you as you pull. Next, turn the dough mound partway around and repeat what you did before. Continue to push, pull, and turn. It takes a little practice to get into the rhythm of kneading. Sprinkle the dough with a tiny bit of water if the dough seems too dry, or a tiny bit of flour if it gets too sticky.

4. Roll the kneaded dough out onto a lightly floured countertop or table until it's ¼ inch (1 cm) thick all over.

5. Place one of the paper pattern pieces on the dough slab and carefully cut the dough with the dull knife, following the edges of the pattern piece. Peel off the tracing paper pattern. Gently lift up the cutout dough and place it on the cookie sheet or pizza pan. Cut out all the other pieces the same way. Peel off the tracing paper pattern after you cut out each piece.

6. Salt dough must be dried very slowly or it will crack. It must also dry completely or it will get mushy and start to rot. **Ask an adult to help you put the pan in a 170°F (76.6°C) oven for one hour.** (If you are using a gas oven, leave the oven door halfway open during the entire hour. Do not use a microwave to dry salt dough.) After an hour, turn the oven up to 200°F (93°C) and dry the dough for 30 minutes more. (If you are using a gas oven, leave the door a quarter of the way open during this baking time.) After 30 minutes, turn the oven up to 250°F (121°C) and dry the dough for another 30 minutes. (If you are using a gas oven, keep the door closed during this baking time.) **Ask an adult to help you take the pan out of the oven.**

7. Let the puzzle pieces cool for 30 minutes, then tap one piece to see if it sounds hollow. If it does, it's completely dry.

8. Paint the pieces with the acrylic paints and let the paint dry. Be sure to wash out your paintbrush when you are done.

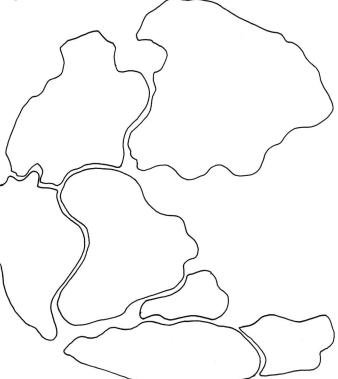

Enlarge pattern by 200%

How Do You Spell Relief? E-a-r-t-h-q-u-a-k-e!

There's a lot of tension in this world, what with the Earth's plates constantly pushing and shoving and grinding into each other, all fighting for position. Usually it's more or less a standoff, with no plate gaining or losing much ground. But sometimes the strain gets to be too much. Rocks in the Earth's crust just can't take it any more. They slip or break apart for a moment (aah, relief!)—and then lock together again in a new position.

That moment of relief for the Earth's crust isn't always relaxing for us, though. When the rocks shift, they release all their built-up energy in the form of shock waves. Those shock waves ripple through the ground and deep into the earth, causing the shake, rattle, and roll we know as an earthquake.

Not all earthquakes cause damage. Hundreds of rock-relieving jerks happen every day along *fault lines*, which are breaks or weak spots in the Earth's crust. In most cases we can barely feel these "miniquakes." But every once in a while a whole lot of tension builds up at a fault line, and when the rocks finally give, they give big. The shock waves are so powerful they make the ground roll and sway and vibrate violently in all directions for dozens or even hundreds of miles. Streets crack. Bridges buckle. Buildings shake themselves to pieces. If a strong earthquake happens near or in an ocean, it might cause a *tsunami* (soo-NAH-mee), or tidal wave. A tidal wave can travel through the sea at almost 500 miles (800 km) per hour. By the time it reaches land, it can be as tall as a 20-story building!

Places near the edges of Earth's crustal plates, such as California, Japan, China, Italy, Greece, and Mexico, get the most earthquakes. But a quake can happen almost anywhere. Some of the strongest earthquakes in North America's history happened in Missouri, right in the middle of the United States, in 1811 and 1812.

By the way, Earth isn't the only shaky place in our solar system. Scientists have recorded thousands of "moonquakes," and several "Marsquakes," too!

Left: Montana earthquake area, 19-foot (6 m) displacement, 1959

Right: This landslide in Anchorage, Alaska, was caused by an earthquake, and destroyed many homes in the city.

RECORD-SETTING EARTHQUAKES

This whole-lot-of-shakin'-goin'-on planet of ours produces between 500,000 and one million earthquakes a year! Most are mild and do little or no harm. From time to time, though, an especially strong earthquake causes a lot of damage.

Here are facts about six Big Ones:

■ **1556, Shaanxi Province, China:** One of the worst disasters ever, this earthquake killed more than 800,000 people.

■ **1755, Lisbon, Portugal:** Scientists think this was one of the strongest earthquakes in history. More than half the city was destroyed and the shocks were felt as far away as Norway. The quake created a giant tidal wave that swept half a mile in from shore and washed away everything in its path.

■ **1906, San Francisco, California:** This famous earthquake created enormous landslides, opened up huge cracks in the ground, and caused many fires. Most of the city's buildings either collapsed or burned to the ground.

■ **1923, Sagami Bay, Japan:** Even though it started underwater, this powerful quake destroyed almost three-quarters of the buildings in Tokyo, 70 miles (112 km) away, and completely demolished Yokohama, 50 miles (80 km) away.

■ **1960, Chile:** Starting in May, this series of enormous earthquakes rocked Chile's coast and flattened most of the buildings in the region. Mud slides and tidal waves caused even more damage. Geologists rank the strongest quake at 9.0 on the Richter scale. That's equal to the explosive power of almost 200 million tons of TNT!

■ **1964, Alaska:** This was the strongest quake in North American history. In some places the ground was lifted 30 feet (9.2 m) higher. Many buildings in Anchorage and surrounding towns were destroyed by the shocks and by the tidal waves it caused.

Seismograph

A SEISMOGRAPH IS A DEVICE THAT
RECORDS VIBRATIONS OF THE EARTH.
IT IS USED TO MEASURE
THE INTENSITY OF EARTH-
QUAKES. WHEN YOU DO
THE EXPERIMENT
DESCRIBED HERE, YOU
WILL GET AN IDEA OF
HOW A SEISMOGRAPH
GIVES SCIENTISTS A
PICTURE OF THE TREMORS
OF THE EARTH DURING
AN EARTHQUAKE.

What You Need

- *Sturdy cardboard box, about 8 by 8 by 11 inches (20 by 20 by 28 cm) or slightly larger*
- *2 pieces of heavy string, each 2 feet (61 cm) long*
- *Scissors*
- *Brick*
- *Awl or large nail*
- *Small block of wood, about 1 by 2 by 3 inches (2.54 by 5 by 8 cm)*

- *Several sheets of typewriter or copier paper*
- *Glue stick*
- *Heavy-duty tape, such as duct tape*
- *3 rubber bands*
- *Pencil with soft lead (number 2) or a stick of vine charcoal (sold at art-supply stores)*

W HAT YOU DO

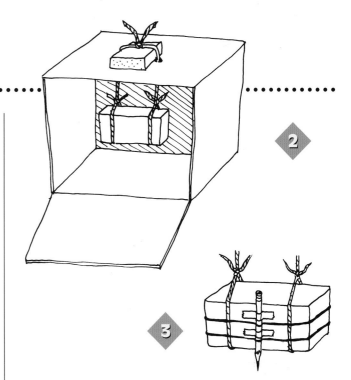

1. Place the box on its side on a table. Tuck in the side and top flaps to strengthen the box. Fold out the bottom flap to form a tray to catch the paper.

2. Tie one string to each side of the brick. If the brick has holes in it, you can tie the strings through the holes in the brick. Tie double knots.

3. Punch two holes, about 4 inches (10 cm) apart, in the center of the top of the box. **1**

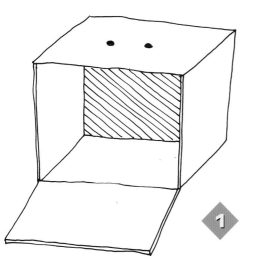

4. Push the ends of the strings through the holes you have poked. You may need to push them first through the holes in the flaps, then through the holes in the actual box. Then, with the brick resting on the bottom of the box, tie the strings together on the top of the box. Pull the strings tight enough so that there is no slack, and tie a double knot.

5. Slide the block of wood under the knot of the string to lift the brick off the bottom of the box. Adjust the string so that the brick hangs evenly. **2**

6. Cut sheets of paper in half and glue them together end to end so that you have a long sheet of paper. You can make this sheet as long as you want, but be sure to make it at least 3 feet (91 cm) long. Roll up the paper when the glue is dry.

7. Slip the roll of paper behind the brick so that the leading edge of paper is on the bottom of the box. Pull out the edge of the paper until it reaches the end of the front flap of cardboard.

8. Use tape and rubber bands to attach the pencil or charcoal to the front flat side of the brick. Make sure that the point comes in contact with the paper so that it can make a mark when the paper is pulled under the brick. Test it out before taping the pencil in position. This is the trickiest part of this project. The pencil must strike the paper hard enough to make a mark, but not so hard as to catch the paper and keep it from being pulled through. You may need to try several different kinds of pencils or charcoal and adjust each several times before you find one that works. Use the rubber bands to hold the pencil or charcoal while you are adjusting it. Once you have found the right position, tape it in place. **3**

9. Place the seismograph on a small table, such as a kitchen table or a coffee table. Ask a friend to cause a table-quake by shaking one of the legs of the table while you slowly pull the paper under the pencil. Pull evenly, and watch your seismograph record the quake. Try different kinds and speeds of shaking and see what results you get.

Volcanoes!

Have you ever given a bottle of soda a really hard shake and then popped the cap? WHOOSH! All those bubbles of gas in the soda push themselves and most of the liquid right out the top.

That's how a volcano erupts, too. *Magma*, which is a mixture of gases and hot molten rock, collects in a chamber deep inside the earth. As more and more magma enters the chamber, more and more pressure builds. The magma pushes hard against the surrounding rock, opening up cracks wherever there are weak spots. Eventually one of the cracks opens almost all the way to the surface. This becomes the volcano's *main tube*, or *pipe*. As the magma rises through the tube and gets closer to the surface, the gases in the molten rock form bubbles, like the bubbles you made when you shook the soda bottle. The bubbles push even harder against the "cap" (the Earth's crust) until—KABOOM! WHOOSH!—they blast through,

blowing a hole right through the surface. Hot steam, ash, and gases come bursting out, pushing huge chunks of rock and big globs of *lava* into the air. Then even more lava spills over the top.

A volcano can erupt many times over the centuries. After each eruption, the lava and ash around the opening, or *crater*, cool and harden. Layer after layer, eruption after eruption, the volcano grows. This is how most of the world's tall, cone-shaped volcanoes, such as Mount Vesuvius in Italy and Mount Fuji in Japan, came to be.

Some volcanoes don't erupt with a huge explosion of dust and gas. Instead, the lava bubbles and boils and spurts to the surface and then flows down the sides, like a huge pot of thick soup that's been left on the stove too long. These are known as "quiet" volcanoes (even though their eruptions can be anything but)! Their lava flows build gently sloping, dome-shaped mounds. Most of Hawaii's great volcanoes, such as Mauna Loa and Kilauea, are dome-shaped volcanoes.

There are nearly 850 active volcanoes in the world. At least 80 are beneath the oceans. When the edge of one ocean plate is pushed beneath another, the rock that has sunk into the mantle melts and rises, bubbling upward into the sea through weak spots in the other plate. When the lava touches water it cools and hardens. In some places so much lava has built up that it sticks far above the water. That's how volcanic islands in the Pacific Ocean, such as the islands of Japan, were formed.

Most volcanoes, like most earthquakes, happen near the edges of Earth's crustal plates. If you mark all the volcanoes in the world on a map and draw lines between them like a connect-the-dots puzzle, you'll have a pretty good sketch of Earth's pushiest plates. There are so many active volcanoes around the edges of the five big plates in the Pacific, that geologists call the area "The Ring of Fire"!

Opposite top: Mount St. Helens eruption with rising ash clouds, Washington, 1980

Opposite bottom: Arching lava fountains. Mount Kilauea, Hawaii, 1970

AMAZING VOLCANO FACTS

■ Erupting volcanoes cause lightning! Ash clouds pick up electrical charges even better than water clouds do. So eruptions often trigger big thunder and lightning storms.

■ In 1883 the volcano Krakatoa, in Indonesia, exploded with one of the most powerful eruptions of all time. Rock pieces were thrown 34 miles (54 km) high. People on the island of Rodrigues, nearly 3,000 miles (4,800 km) away, heard the volcano and described the sound as "the roar of heavy guns." Within two weeks, ash from the volcano had completely encircled the Earth!

■ The largest active volcano on earth is Hawaii's Mauna Loa, a dome volcano only 13,680 feet (4,209 m) high but more than 75 miles (120 km) long and 30 miles (29 km) wide.

■ The largest known volcano isn't on Earth at all. It's on Mars! The volcano Olympus Mons is 17 miles (27 km) high—that's three times taller than Mount Everest, the tallest mountain on Earth!

Lava drapery hardened over a sea cliff, formed during an eruption of Kilauea Volcano in Hawaii

EXPLODING *Volcaño*

This is the popular soda and vinegar exploding volcano experiment, with a couple of new twists. Gather a few friends to watch when you fire off your volcano!

What You Need

- *Small glass or plastic bottle with a narrow neck*
- *Piece of cardboard, about 12 by 15 inches (30 by 38 cm)*
- *Modeling clay*
- *Funnel or piece of heavy paper to roll into a funnel*
- *Measuring cup*
- *1 pound (454 g) box of bicarbonate of soda (baking soda)*
- *Red food coloring*
- *1 quart (946 ml) bottle of vinegar (any kind will do)*
- *Spoon*

HAT YOU DO

1. Remove the lid from the bottle if it has one and stand the bottle in the middle of the piece of cardboard.

2. Use flat slabs of clay to model a volcano around the bottle. Leave the mouth of the bottle open.

3. Use the funnel (or the piece of paper rolled into a cone) to pour about ¼ cup (50 g) of baking soda into the mouth of the bottle. The amount you pour in will depend on how big the bottle is. You want to fill the bottle about halfway.

4. Pour a few drops of red food coloring into ½ cup (118.3 ml) of vinegar and stir or swirl it to mix it.

5. Now the excitement begins! Place the volcano on a countertop or table that is okay to get wet. You could also try putting the volcano in the bottom of an empty bathtub or someplace flat outdoors. Carefully pour some vinegar into the mouth of the volcano—and stand back!

6. You can make several explosions without adding more soda simply by pouring in more vinegar each time the "lava" stops flowing. Notice where the lava flows. Does it flow in the same place each time? Does it flow in different places? Why might that be? What effect would this volcano have on the land, plants, buildings, and people nearby? In which ways is this model like a real volcano? In which ways is it different?

7. When you are finished using the model, lift the clay from the cardboard, and gently pull on the bottle until it comes out. Then rinse out the bottle and dry it. Pat the clay mountain shape dry, and replace the bottle. You can use this volcano many times.

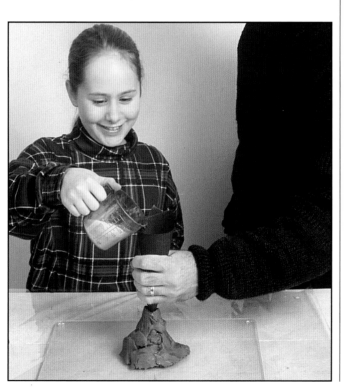

Nature's "Tea Kettles"

Our planet's insides are so fiery that in some places the heat just naturally boils out. Water from rain or underground streams flows through a spot where Earth's mantle is especially close to the surface. The rocks there are hot enough to make the water hot, too. These places are called *hot springs*. The steaming water that bubbles to the surface is great for bathing. People come from all over the world to special resorts, such as the one in Hot Springs, Arkansas.

A *geyser* is a different sort of hot spring. You wouldn't want to take a bath in one! Instead of bubbling to the surface, the water in a geyser comes out in a rush of scalding steam. Then the geyser quiets down again. More water collects in an underground chamber to replace the water that steamed out. The rocks around the chamber heat the new water until, eventually, it becomes super hot and erupts too. Some geysers, such as Old Faithful in Yellowstone

Above: Minerva Hot Springs. Yellowstone National Park, Wyoming

Left: Riverside Geyser in eruption. Yellowstone National Park, Wyoming

National Park, erupt "faithfully" over and over again, spitting out between 10,000 to 12,000 gallons (37,850 to 45,420 l) of hot vaporized water every 30 to 90 minutes! Most geysers, though, aren't as predictable. Some take days, weeks, or even years to erupt again.

Most of the world's hot springs and geysers are in only three countries: New Zealand, Iceland, and the United States. People in Iceland are especially good at using the naturally hot water to make their lives easier. Water heated by the Earth is piped directly to radiators and hot water tanks in homes and office buildings. Almost 100 percent of the city of Reykjavik, the capital of Iceland, is heated with hot springs.

PEBBLE MOSAIC
Flowerpot

PEBBLES AND PLANTS ARE MADE FOR EACH OTHER. THEIR COLORS LOOK GOOD TOGETHER, AND THEIR BEAUTIFUL ORGANIC SHAPES REMIND US OF THE NATURAL WORLD. TRY COVERING A SMALL FLOWERPOT WITH SOME OF YOUR FAVORITE PEBBLES.

WHAT YOU DO

1. Cover your work surface with two sheets of newspaper. Make a small puddle of glue on one piece of newspaper. Lay out a few pebbles. Use your finger to place a blob of glue on the flat side of each pebble. Let the glue dry and thicken for a few minutes.

2. Turn the flower pot upside down on the other piece of newspaper. Place gluey pebbles next to each other all over the pot. Begin by placing the rim pebbles. If you build up from the rim, the pebbles will rest on the ones beneath them and will not slide. If they begin to slide, let the glue dry a little longer. Sometimes it will be necessary to hold a pebble in place for a few minutes until the glue sets. It helps to lightly tap each pebble with the tip of your fingernail, much like a brick mason taps each brick, to help it sit more firmly in the mortar.

3. Let the pot dry for several hours. The glue should dry clear: it won't be necessary to clean up any extra blobs or drips.

4. Pot your favorite plant in its nice new home.

WHAT YOU NEED

- *Old newspapers*
- *White waterproof craft glue*
- *Collection of pebbles, preferably ones that have at least one flat side*
- *Small clay flower pot*

Left: Bridal Veil Falls, an outstanding example of a waterfall flowing from a hanging valley. Yosemite National Park, California

Opposite: Grand Canyon in the morning light. Grand Canyon National Park, Arizona

Mountains High, Valleys Low

You might say that Mother Nature just can't make up her mind: First she builds mountains, then tears them down and scatters the remains.

On page 18 we saw how the tectonic plates of the crust move and collide with each other and give birth to mountains. When one plate dives deep, the rock gets hot in the mantle and then sizzles up to make volcanic mountains, like the Andes in South America. Plates also make mountains when they collide and buckle their edges, like a rumpled rug. This is what raised the Alps in Europe and the Himalayas in Asia.

Mountains are also born in the ocean. The Hawaiian Islands, such as Mount Kilauea, are the tops of submarine volcanoes that have risen several miles out of the sea floor.

Almost as fast as mountains rise up, *erosion*, the world's demolition expert, wears them back down.

The most important tool of erosion is water. Rainfall seeps into rocks and helps them break apart and dissolve; ice expands when it freezes and forces rock apart. Streams and rivers carry rock particles downstream and dump them in lakes or oceans, sometimes hundreds of miles away.

The higher the mountains, the faster the demolition. The Himalayas, including Mount Everest, are very steep and young mountains (about 45 million years old). They are still rising today and eroding very fast. The Appalachian mountains, which run from Alabama to Newfoundland, are old mountains (nearly 400 million years old) which have been lowered and smoothed by erosion.

If you've ever seen the Grand Canyon, you've witnessed what erosion can do in 15 or 20 million years! The Colorado River has cut through rock more than a mile deep, breaking many millions of tons into sand

and carrying it downstream into Lake Mead, which was built in 1936 to create Hoover Dam.

Most erosion happens during big floods, when a mass of mud may suddenly slide down a bank; or a landslide may bring down part of a mountain; or a river may gouge into its banks. A fast stream can cut into solid rock like a sandblaster, scouring the bedrock with its load of sand, gravel, and rock.

The land is also reshaped by *glaciers*, mountain-sized masses of ice that flow downhill a few inches or feet every day. Glaciers act like huge, slow-motion snowplows, pushing sand and gravel and rocks before them, smoothing off hills, polishing solid rock, and carving U-shaped valleys through mountains! When they stop and melt, they leave piles of sediment called *moraines*. Cape Cod, Massachusetts, and Long Island, New York, are moraines bulldozed hundreds of miles southward by glaciers.

Glaciers can also make the kind of landscape we see on picture postcards. The last Ice Age in Europe and North America, which ended about 10,000 years ago, left behind rolling hills, small lakes, and fertile fields. They also brought several feet of rich topsoil to the American Midwest—which makes midwestern farmers happy, but doesn't thrill Canadian farmers!

A third powerful tool of erosion is wind, which can quickly reshape the face of the Earth. A powerful windstorm can move enough sand to bury a house; wind-blown sand can chip away at solid rock. In large dust storms, a cubic mile (4 cubic km) of air may carry 4,000 tons (4,408 metric tons) of dust! Parts of the central United States are covered by more than 25 feet (7.7 m) of wind-carried soil called *loess*.

MOUNTAIN Building

HERE ARE THREE EXPERIMENTS THAT DEMONSTRATE THE PROCESS BY WHICH MANY MOUNTAIN RANGES WERE CREATED. OF COURSE, IT TAKES HUNDREDS AND HUNDREDS OF YEARS FOR A MOUNTAIN RANGE TO DEVELOP, BUT THESE SIMPLE EXPERIMENTS WILL LET YOU IMAGINE HOW GREAT SLABS OF THE EARTH'S CRUST MOVING TOWARD EACH OTHER COULD PUSH UP MOUNTAINS.

WHAT YOU NEED

- *2 large chunks of clay (either ceramic clay or plasticine), each twice as big as your fist*
- *Rolling pin*
- *Dull table knife*
- *2 pieces of aluminum foil, each about 5 inches (13 cm) long*
- *Fat dowel or a piece of an old broomstick*

WHAT YOU DO

1. Work the lumps of clay with your hands until they are soft and easy to bend and shape.

2. Roll each chunk out until it is about 8 inches (20 cm) long, 4 inches (10 cm) wide, and 2 inches (5 cm) high. Trim the chunks with the knife so that they look like bricks.

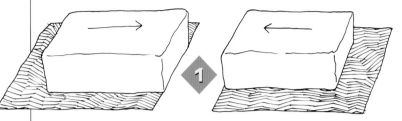

3. Place each clay brick onto the edge of a piece of aluminum foil. Each brick will represent a land mass.

4. Place the two land masses—each riding on its aluminum foil plate—about 12 inches (30 cm) apart on a smooth table or countertop.

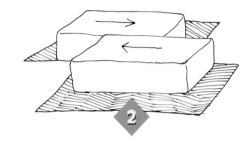

5. For the first experiment, hold each land mass at its far end and slam them together as hard as you can. **1** Try this several times. Describe what happens. Describe how the clay after the collision is like the edge of a continent that has had a collision with another continent. In what ways was your experiment like real life? In what ways was it different?

6. Separate the clay and form it into bricks again. For the second experiment, place the long side of each brick along an edge of its aluminum foil. **2** Push the two bricks so that they brush against each other as they travel past each other. Describe what happens. How is the edge of the clay like an edge of a continent that has had another land mass slide alongside it?

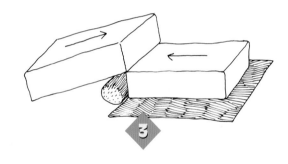

7. Often, one land mass is heavier than the other, and it sinks under the lighter land mass as the two collide. In the third experiment, you will use a dowel to lift one clay brick over the other. First, make the clay into two bricks again. Sit one of them on a piece of aluminum foil. Place the other brick facing the first brick, but with one of its short end tilted up so that it rests on the dowel. **3** Slide the two bricks toward each other and jam them together. What happens as they hit each other? How is this collision different from the first or second one that you tried. What kind of land forms would be the result of a collision like this?

LANDFORM Pop-Up BOOK

It's fun to discover ways to use pop-ups to show different landforms. Here are directions for four different kinds of pop-ups. Try combining them or changing them to create your own book of landforms.

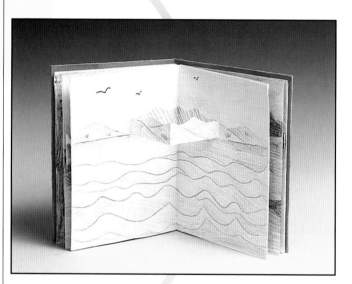

What You Need

- *Unlined white paper, such as typing or copier paper, 8½ by 11 inches (22 by 28 cm)*
- *Pencil*
- *Scissors*
- *Ruler*
- *Glue stick*
- *Colored pencils or crayons*
- *1 sheet of colored construction paper, 9 by 12 inches (23 by 30.5 cm)*
- *Paper clip*

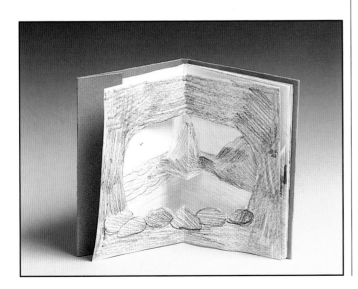

1. Decide which landforms you want to include in your book. Some ideas to start with are a mountain, hills, a butte, a river valley, a sea cave, stalactites and stalagmites, cliffs, a volcano, or sand dunes. Make a simple drawing of the landform on white paper and decide which kind of pop-up would best show it.

2. Fold a sheet of white paper in half from top to bottom and cut it along the fold line. You will now have two pieces of paper, each measuring 5½ by 8½ inches (14 by 22 cm). Fold each of these in half, as in figure **1**. This is the first step in making any of the four pop-ups that follow.

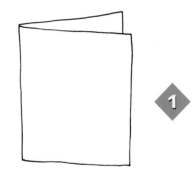

To make a pop-up from the center of the page:

a. Draw a straight line from the folded edge halfway across the page. Make this line where you want the bottom of your pop-up to be. **2**

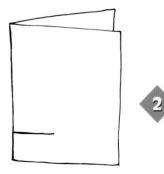

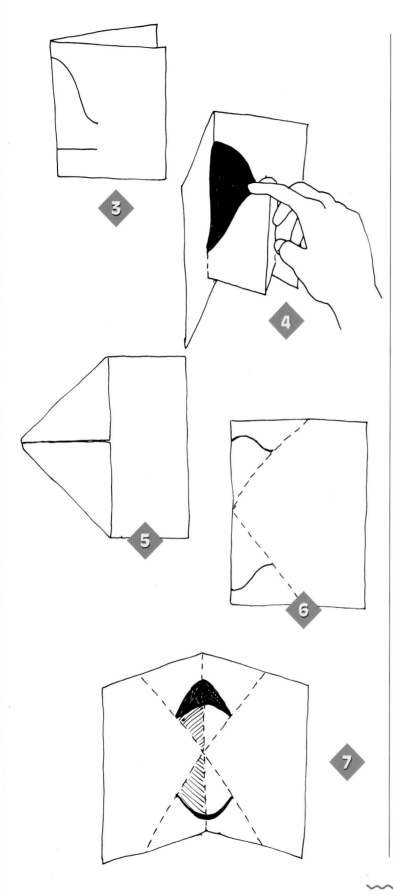

b. Draw the top edge of the pop-up in whatever shape it needs to be to show the landform you are making. Don't go past the middle of the page. Remember that you are drawing half of the landform. So, for example, you would draw a mountain like this: **3**

c. Cut along both lines.

d. Open the page and gently pull the pop-up toward you. **4**

e. Close the page with the pop-up folded on the inside and press to crease all the folds.

To make two pop-ups from the center of the page:

a. Fold the top and bottom corners of the folded side of the paper down so that they meet, forming two triangles. **5**

b. Unfold the triangles and draw the top edge of the pop-ups from the folded edges of the paper to the fold lines you have just made. **6**

c. Cut along the lines you have drawn.

d. Open the page and gently pull the pop-ups toward you along the fold lines you made in step a. **7**. You will have to reverse the direction of the folds.

e. Close the page with the pop-ups folded to the inside. Press hard to make sharp creases.

To make a pop-up that sticks out past the edge of the paper:

a. Fold a triangle down from the top corner of the folded edge, like this: **8**

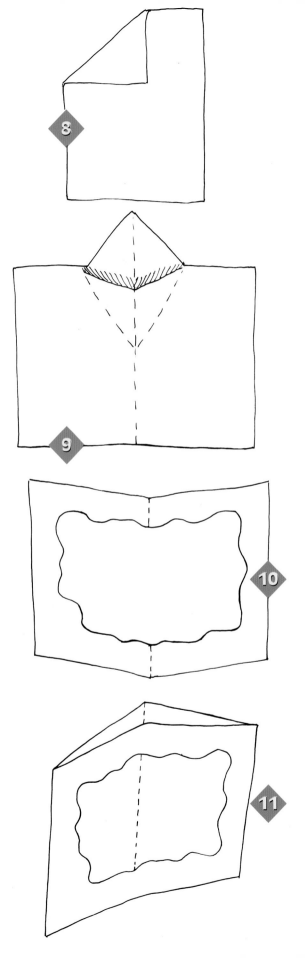

b. Open the page and gently pull the triangle to the inside. Close the page again, with the triangle inside. Press to crease the folds.

c. From a scrap of paper, cut out a triangle with a 2- to 2½-inch (5 to 6.5 cm) base and fold it in half.

d. Glue the cutout triangle to the triangle that is folded inside the page. Match the fold lines. **9**

e. Close the page. If the new triangle sticks out, trim the tip so that it fits completely inside the folded page.

f. Draw the landform on the two triangles. You may want to trim the tip to make it some other shape to suit your landform.

To make an opening that comes forward:

a. Trim 1 inch (2.5 cm) off one short edge of the sheet of paper. Fold the paper in half.

b. Draw the opening that you want (a cave? a rock arch?). Cut out the opening, being sure to leave the edges around the opening uncut. **10**

c. Put a ½-inch (1.5 cm) strip of glue along each of the two side edges of the pop-up on the back side of the paper. Glue these edges to the edges of another sheet of 5½-by-8½-inch (14 by 22 cm) folded paper. Since the cutout page is shorter than the underneath page, you won't be able to open this pop-up completely, but as you open it, the top page will come forward. **11**

d. Try making another pop-up in the inside of this pop-up. You will make the inside pop-up just like any other pop-up. It's a good idea to make the inside pop-up before gluing the front pop-up to the inside page. Glue the inside pop-up to its back page first, then glue the front pop-up to the inside page.

3. **For all pop-ups, this is the next step:** Glue the pop-up page inside another folded page of 5½-by-8½-inch (14 by 22 cm) white paper. When you are gluing, be sure to put glue everywhere except on the back of the pop-up part.

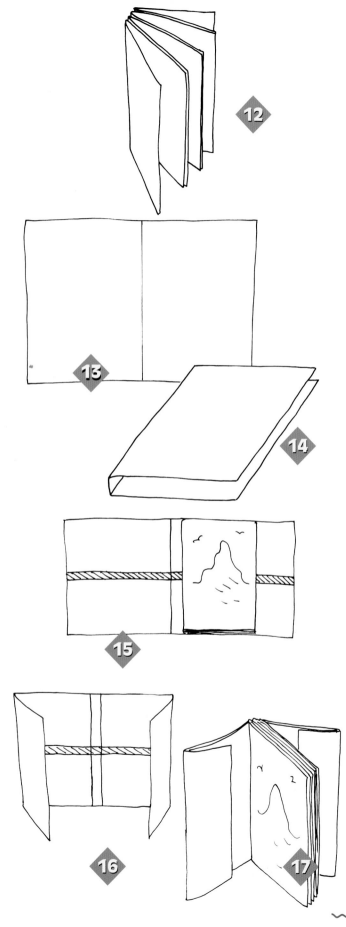

4. Open the pop-up page and finish drawing and coloring the landform as well as the page around it to make an environment for the landform. Color the paper that shows behind the pop-up so that it blends in with the scene you have drawn.

5. To make a book out of all the pop-up pages, begin by stacking all the folded pop-ups in the order you want them to be in the book. Put glue all over the outside back page of the first pop-up, and then lay it on top of the outside front page of the next pop-up. Repeat this step until all the pages are glued together. **12**

6. Fold two blank 5½-by-8½-inch (14 by 22 cm) sheets of paper. Glue one to the top and one to the bottom of the stack of pages.

7. To make a cover for your book, lay a sheet of colored construction paper on the table. Use a ruler to find the center, and draw a line to mark the center of the paper. **13**

8. Use the paper clip and ruler to score two lines, each ¼ inch (1 cm) away from the center line on either side. To score, simply press hard with the rounded end of the paper clip. Scoring makes it easier to fold stiff paper. Fold the paper along the scored lines to make a spine for the book. **14**

9. Slip the stack of pages inside the cover, pushing it all the way in against the spine. Open the cover, keeping the pages in place. Use the ruler and paper clip to score lines across the top and bottom of the stack of pages. Fold the cover along these scored lines. **15**

10. Again slip the stack of pages inside the cover against the spine. Score a line along the outer edge of the pages, then move the page stack over to the other side of the spine, and score another line along the outer edge of the stack. Fold the cover along each of these two newly scored lines. **16**

11. Slip the first and last pages of the page stack into the space inside each cover fold over. **17** Decorate the cover to finish the book.

The Map Makers

*L*ook at a regular highway map: You can see where roads, towns, and cities are, along with a few really big natural features, like lakes and rivers. But a highway map doesn't give a clue about hills or valleys, let alone the rocks below the surface.

So geologists make their own maps. It's sort of like making a map of your backyard. You'd show the lawn, bushes, driveway, tree house, and fence. A geologist's backyard is much bigger, and a geological map shows whole rock formations—the kind of rock, how thick it is, how it rises or falls, and what kind of rock lives next door.

The map may have different colors for different kinds of rocks. Granite might be red; shale, green; sandstone, sandy; limestone, light blue; marble, dark blue, and so on.

And it will have curvy lines all over it. These are *contour lines*, which show whether the land is steep or level. Every point on a contour line is at the same altitude above sea level. The line next to it is either higher or lower by a number that's written on the map—usually an amount between 20 and 200 feet (6 and 61 m). When the land is steep, like on a mountainside, the lines are very close together. When the land is level, the lines are far apart.

Geologists draw little symbols to show whether rocks are tilted up or down (this is called *dip*) and the direction of dip (*strike*). Dip and strike are important because they show how the crustal plates have shifted and heaved whole rock formations and mountains around. Rocks that used to lie level may be tilted steeply and even turned on end. That's like turning your floor into a wall!

There are other symbols geologists use to mark things: mines, folded rocks, mineral veins, loose rocks or pebbles, landslides, gemstones, fossils, grooves cut in rocks by glaciers, and other interesting features.

What a geological detective really wants to look at is an *outcrop* of *bedrock*, the thick, unbroken rock of the crust that lies under everything else. But how can you

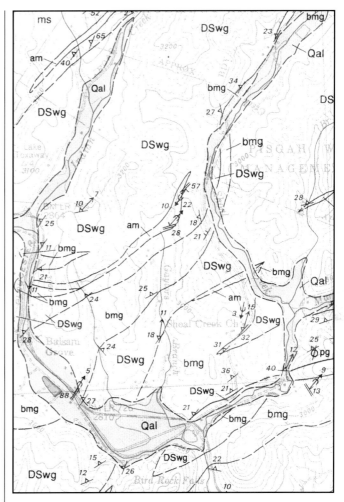

see bedrock when it's hidden under plants, soil, sand, water, and buildings? Unless you want to do a lot of digging, you have to search for an outcrop where bedrock pokes through the surface. You can also use places where someone else has done the digging for you— highway and railroad cuts, quarries, and abandoned mines. Other good places to see bedrock are cliffs and some river banks. Once you find bedrock in one place, you can compare it to other places you find bedrock and begin filling the blanks on your map.

Why go to all the trouble to make a geological map? This is how a geologist tries to understand how the surface of the Earth got to be the way it is.

You can get an idea of what a geological map looks like in most libraries, or you can order them from the U.S. Geological Survey or other public agency.

MEASURING a Slope

Have you ever wondered how high a hill is? One way to find out is to use a process called leveling. This is a very old way of measuring the height of a slope. In earlier days, people actually used this method to measure the height of some of the highest mountains. Here's how you and a friend can use a homemade instrument to measure a slope.

What You Need

- Quart-size (946 ml) glass jar with a lid, half filled with water
- Wide rubber band
- Pointed stick about 2 feet (61 cm) long
- Notebook
- Pencil
- Tape measure

WHAT YOU DO

1. Place the jar of water on a level table or level ground. When the water stops sloshing around, carefully place the rubber band around the jar at exactly the level of the water.

2. You'll need a friend to help with the next steps. Stand at the bottom of the slope you want to measure. Give your friend the stick. Hold the jar in front of your face so that you look straight across the water. Use the rubber band to see when the water has stopped sloshing and is level. (Make sure the water level and the rubber band are in the same place. If the top of the water is in a different place from the rubber band, tip the jar until they are in the same place. Now look across the leveled water.)

3. While you are looking across the water, spot a place on the slope, and ask your friend to put the tip of the stick there as a marker.

4. Record "1" in your notebook.

5. Now climb up the slope and stand where the point of the stick is touching the ground. Place your feet on either side of that spot, and look through the leveled water for the next place on the slope to mark. Ask your friend to move the stick to the new mark. Record another mark in your notebook.

6. Repeat step 5 until you reach the top of the hill or as far up the slope as you want to measure.

7. Add up all your marks and write the sum in your notebook.

8. Ask your friend to help you use the tape measure to measure the distance from your eyes to the ground beneath your feet. Multiply the number of marks you recorded by the distance between your eyes and the ground. The answer is the height of the slope you just measured.

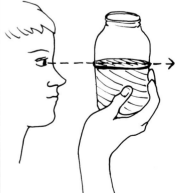

MAKING A Topographic MAP

A TOPOGRAPHIC MAP SHOWS MOUNTAINS AND VALLEYS, HIGH PLACES AND LOW PLACES. PEOPLE WHO KNOW HOW TO READ THESE MAPS CAN TELL BY LOOKING AT ONE JUST HOW STEEP A CERTAIN HILL IS. THEY CAN PLAN THE EASIEST PLACE TO BUILD A ROAD THAT MUST CROSS A MOUNTAIN RANGE OR THEY CAN USE THE MAP TO HELP FIND THE BEST PLACE TO BUILD A LOOKOUT TOWER. THIS PROJECT WILL HELP YOU UNDERSTAND HOW TO READ A TOPOGRAPHIC MAP.

WHAT YOU NEED

- *Lump of clay twice as big as your fist*
- *Piece of cardboard or large tile, 12 by 12 inches (31 by 31 cm)*
- *Wire coat hanger*
- *2-foot (61 cm) long piece of dental floss*
- *2 sticks, each about 3 inches (7.6 cm) long*
- *Ruler*
- *Piece of white paper*
- *Pencil*

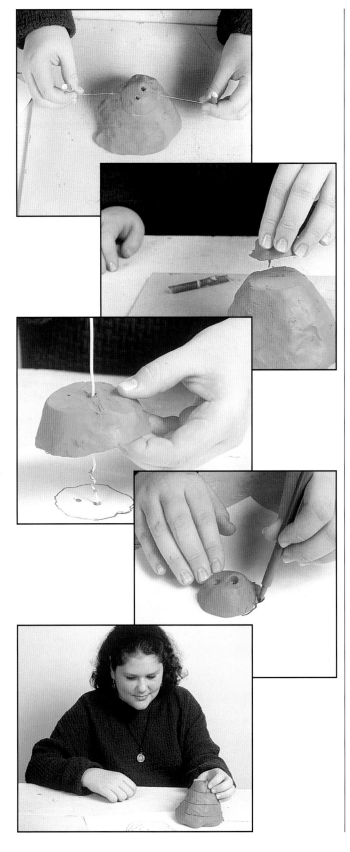

1. Make a mountain out of the clay and place it on the cardboard.

2. Straighten out the coat hanger. Use one end to poke two holes straight down through the center of the mountain. Make sure your two holes go all the way through the mountain.

3. Tie each end of the dental floss to one of the short sticks and stretch the dental floss until it is taut. Hold onto the handles and use the dental floss to cut through the mountain around 1 inch down from the peak.

4. Remove this clay slice and place it on the paper. Use the pencil to carefully trace around it. Push the pencil through one of the holes in the clay and make a dot on the paper; do the same with the other hole. Put the slice aside, but don't squash it. You'll need it again later.

5. Cut a second slice, 1 inch (2.5 cm) down from the first. Lay the second slice over the tracing of the first one, being careful to place the holes in the second slice over the dots on the paper. To line up the holes precisely, poke the coat hanger through one of the holes in the slice until it touches one of the dots on the paper; do the same with the other hole. Carefully trace around the second slice. Your tracing will form a circle outside the tracing of the first slice.

6. Cut as many more slices as you can, each 1 inch (2.5 cm) down from the one before it. Line up the holes with the dots and trace each as you cut it.

7. When you have traced all the slices, stack them back up in order on the cardboard. Be sure the holes line up.

8. Compare the topographic map you have made to the model mountain. Why are some of the traced lines closer together than others? What kind of slope gives you lines that are close together? What kind gives lines that are far apart? On your topographic map, where are the steepest slopes? Where would be the best place to build a trail to climb to the top of the mountain?

Self-Folding MAP

THIS IS A POCKET-SIZE MAP THAT NOT ONLY UNFOLDS EASILY BUT ALSO FOLDS ITSELF BACK UP. YOU CAN DRAW YOUR OWN MAP ON IT OR GLUE ON A MAP THAT YOU WANT TO USE ON A ROCK COLLECTING TRIP.

WHAT YOU NEED

- *A sheet of heavy-weight paper for the map cover*
- *Pencil*
- *Ruler*
- *Scissors*
- *Sheet of plain white paper, 8½ by 11 inches (22 by 28 cm) to use for the map (If you want to use a map that is already drawn, cut it to 8½ by 11 inches (22 by 28 cm) and use it in place of the plain white paper.)*
- *Glue stick*

WHAT YOU DO

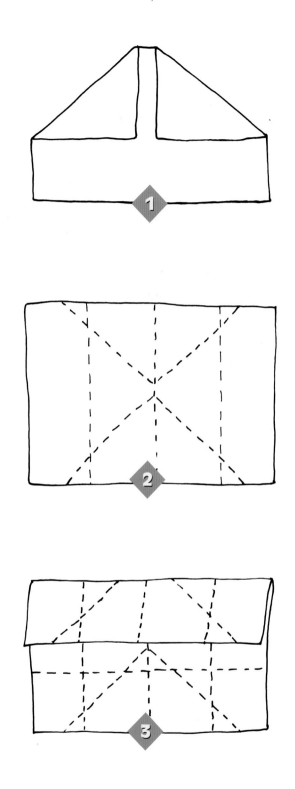

1. Use the pencil and ruler to mark the cover sheet so that it is 5 by 11 inches (13 by 28 cm), and then cut it out. Put this sheet aside for now.

2. Fold the plain white paper in half so that it measures 5½ by 8½ inches (14 by 28 cm). If you are using a map that is already drawn, fold it so that the map is on the inside.

3. Turn the paper so that the fold runs across the top. Fold the two top corners down as though you were making a hat. Be sure to leave a ¼-inch (1 cm) space between the two flaps. **1**

4. Press all the creases, then unfold the paper completely, with an 11-inch (28 cm) edge at the top. Keep the map side facing up if you are using a map that is already drawn. About 3½ inches (9 cm) in from the left side, make a fold that goes from top to bottom. Press the crease.

5. Repeat step 4 on the right side. Unfold the paper again. You should have creases that look like **2**.

6. Two inches (5 cm) down from the top, make a fold that goes evenly across the paper. The middle of the top should come to the point of the bottom V. **3**

7. Repeat step 6 two inches (5 cm) up from the bottom.

8. Unfold the paper, keeping the map side up if you are using a map that is already drawn. It should have creases that look like figure **4**.

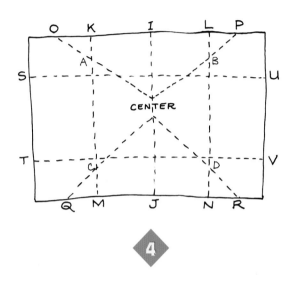

9. Now that you have made all the creases you will need, it's time to refold the paper. You will have to fold a few of the creases back in the opposite direction, but you will be using the same fold lines. Here's how to do it: Pull points I and J so that they come up off of the table while points A, B, C, and D stay on the table. Crease again the folds that go from the center to I and from the center to J, so that points I and J lift up and bring with them creases I-center and J-center.

10. Now lift points O, P, Q, and R up toward you one at a time, reversing the creases that go from O to A and from Q to C.

11. At this stage of folding, points I, J, O, P, Q, and R should all be lifting off the table. Hold the paper with your left hand at point I and your right hand at point J. Push these two points towards each other and down toward one side. The rest of the points should also come towards each other, and one whole side of the paper should be trying to fold over on top of the other side. You should help the paper do just that. Let go of points I and J and press the side that wants to be on top onto the rest of the paper. **5**

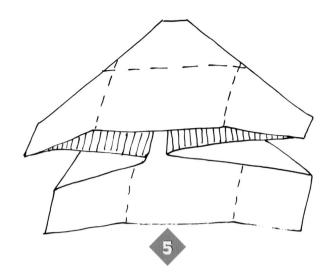

12. Fold and unfold the map a few times to be sure it works, fixing creases as necessary. To glue the map into the cover, first fold it up. Then put glue all over the outside of the top side of the folded map. Open up the cover paper. Press the flattened point of the sticky side of the folded map into the fold of the cover. **6** Press the map to help it stick to the cover.

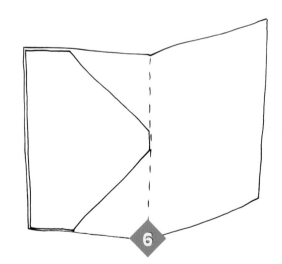

13. Now put glue all over the other surface of the folded map.

14. Bring the unglued cover of the map folder over on top of the glued surface and press down hard to help stick the glue. Press the map under a heavy book while the glue is drying. If you haven't yet drawn a map on the paper, do so now, or wait until you are out walking in the area you want to map.

Where Do Rocks Come From?

By now you know that Earth is a very active place. The crustal plates scrape and collide and dive beneath each other, causing earthquakes and volcanoes, and building mountains. As they do this, the plates play a nonstop game with the Earth's rocks that is as dynamic as a great video game, but much s-l-o-w-e-r! Part of the game is to change all three kinds of rocks—igneous, sedimentary, and metamorphic—into other kinds of rocks.

In this chapter we'll see how rocks can be created deep in Earth's mantle, raised slowly to the surface, destroyed by water and wind, and created again, and again, and again. These changes are part of what is called the *rock cycle*.

The rock cycle moves in such slow motion that geologists measure those movements in *geologic time*. To a geologist, a million years is just a blink of an eye. In fact, there have been about 4,500 million-year blinks since the Earth was formed! With that kind of time to play with, it's not hard to imagine how a rock formed at the bottom of the ocean can end up on a mountaintop—many millions of years later.

The flat, neat layers on top were formed when molten rock erupted through volcanoes and then cooled and hardened. Below these layers are much thicker deposits of eroded shale, formed when silt and mud sank to the bottom of a lake or ocean and became rock. Colorado's Mount Garfield

Granite PAPER

WHEN YOU STOP TO LOOK
CAREFULLY AT ROCKS, YOU'LL
BEGIN TO NOTICE AND APPRECIATE
THEIR MANY BEAUTIFUL COLORS
AND INTERESTING SHAPES AND
TEXTURES. THIS PAPER IS
DESIGNED TO LOOK LIKE GRANITE,
WITH ITS MULTICOLORED SURFACE.
THE TOP PHOTOGRAPH SHOWS A
GOOD EXAMPLE OF GRANITE.

WHAT YOU NEED

- *Rough cement sidewalk or a concrete block*
  or any flat concrete surface
- *Colored pencils or crayons*
- *Piece of granite or a photograph*
  of a piece of granite
- *Plain white paper*

Sweetwater Granite, showing structures stripped of outer layers. Granite Mountains, Wyoming

WHAT YOU DO

1. Brush off any loose pieces of concrete or other debris from the concrete surface you plan to use.

2. Choose three or four colors of crayon or colored pencil that you can see in the piece of granite or the photograph of granite. Lay a sheet of white paper on the concrete.

3. Use one hand to hold the paper firmly in place while you gently and evenly color over the entire area that you want to look like granite. Use a medium or light color for this first layer.

4. Move the paper slightly so the little concrete bumps will be in different places and then color with a different color. Be sure to hold the paper in place and to color evenly.

5. Continue moving the paper and then holding and coloring it with the different colors that you see in the rock you are using as a model. Stop when the paper looks like granite.

6. Use your granite paper to cover books (see page 8), to wrap gifts, or as note cards.

PEBBLE Race

Small flat pebbles make nice markers for games. They can be used to play tic-tac-toe as well as race games, such as the one described here.

1

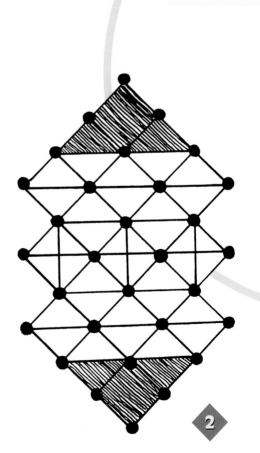

2

Enlarge game board pattern on a copier by 200%

WHAT YOU NEED

- Old sock without a hole in the toe
- Scissors
- Shoelace or leather thong, about 12 inches (31 cm) long
- Piece of paper, 10 by 10 inches (25 by 25 cm)
- Pencil
- Colored markers
- Piece of lightweight cardboard, 10 by 10 inches (25 by 25 cm)
- Glue stick
- 6 flat, round dark-colored pebbles
- 6 flat, round light-colored pebbles

WHAT YOU DO

1. First make a bag in which to keep your markers. Cut off the toe end of the sock, leaving the sock as long as possible without including the heel. Make a straight cut across the sock so that the heel is cut off.

2. Cut eight small holes around the cut edge. These are for the lacing. **1**

3. Thread the shoelace or leather thong through the holes, and your bag is ready to use.

4. Enlarge the game board pattern **2** as indicated. Color over the game board dots and lines with a black marker, and color the two triangular "home bases" with a colored marker.

5. Glue the paper to the piece of cardboard.

To play Pebble Race:

〰 Two people at a time can play Pebble Race. One player places the dark-colored pebbles on the dots of his or her home base, and the other player places the light-colored pebbles on the dots of his or her home base.

〰 The winner is the first player to get at least three pebbles across the board and safely into the other player's home base. The pebbles may be placed on any of the six dots that are in the home base.

〰 Players take turns making their moves. Pebbles can be moved only along the lines that connect the dots, and they can be moved only in a forward or sideways direction. They may not be moved backwards.

〰 A pebble can jump a pebble that is next to it as long as it follows the lines that connect the dots and moves in a straight line during the jump. If a player jumps his or her own pebble, the jumped pebble stays where it is. But if a player jumps the other person's pebble, the jumper captures the jumped pebble and removes it from the board. It is okay to jump more than one pebble at a time, and the pebbles jumped can be from both players. In other words, I can jump (and capture) your pebble, and if that move puts me next to my own pebble, I can jump it, too, in order to move my pebble farther along the board.

〰 A player can lose three pebbles and still win the game, but once someone captures more than three of the other player's pebbles, the other player can't win. Play should continue, however, because it is still possible for the second player to capture the other player's pebbles so that he or she can't win, either, causing the game to end in a draw.

Igneous, Pop! . . . .

Did you ever put a stone into a campfire? It doesn't melt, does it? But inside the Earth's mantle it's hot enough to melt rock! Only when this hot liquid rock gets near the cool surface does it harden (or *crystallize*) to form *igneous rock*. Igneous (IG-nee-us) comes from the Latin word for fire.

In Chapter One we learned that plates of the Earth's crust can dive down into the red-hot mantle. If they dive deep enough, they melt into magma. After a long time, this liquid magma may rise through older, harder rocks toward the surface—as fast as a mile a day.

Some of the magma pops right through the surface as a volcano. But most of it stops underground to form huge masses called *plutons* (named for Pluto, the Roman god of the underworld). Plutons take thousands or even millions of years to cool. While they're cooling, they heat everything around them, including the groundwater. This water may turn to steam and shoot up as geysers, like Old Faithful in Yellowstone National Park.

Magma is a very hot, thick soup of water, carbon dioxide, silicon, aluminum, iron and many other dissolved chemicals. When it cools, it can form many kinds of igneous rock. The magma under oceans usually produces *basalt*, whose dark colors can be seen in pictures of Hawaiian volcanoes. Magma rising under continents

Devils Tower, an igneous intrusive body exposed by erosion. Devils Tower National Monument, Wyoming

usually produces *granite*, which is lighter-colored and grainier than basalt. The volcanoes around the Pacific "rim of fire" come from *andesite magma*, which is partway between basalt and granite; andesite was named after the Andes mountains.

As a rock cools, it grows crystals; the slower a rock cools, the larger its crystals. Plutons cool slowly, because they are deep in the Earth, and plutonic crystals may be large enough to see by eye; some are several inches or feet long. Volcanic rock cools quickly in the ocean or atmosphere, and its crystals may be too small to see. Some lava cools very fast when it is thrown into the air, making a dark glass called *obsidian* which has no grains at all.

Here's a puzzle: If most granite is formed underground in plutons, why do we see so many granite rocks lying around on the ground? The answer is that igneous rocks like granite are very hard, but the sedimentary rock above is softer. Eventually this softer rock breaks down in the rain and wind, exposing the granite below.

Igneous rocks that have been smoothed by water

SMALL ROUND PEBBLES HAVE
BEEN USED FOR GAMES FOR
HUNDREDS OF YEARS. A
PAINTING ON THE WALL OF
AN ANCIENT ROMAN HOUSE
SHOWS PEOPLE PLAYING A
GAME WITH SMALL STONES.
THE GAMES DESCRIBED IN
THIS PROJECT ARE SIMILAR
TO THOSE PLAYED LONG AGO.

GAME
Pebbles

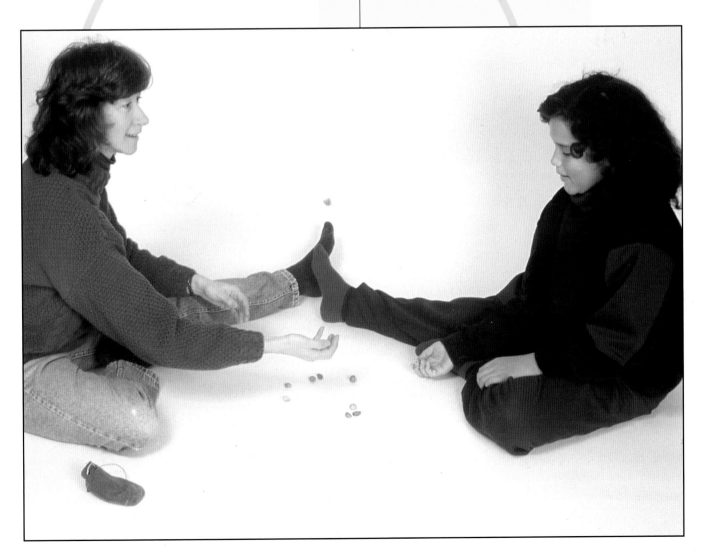

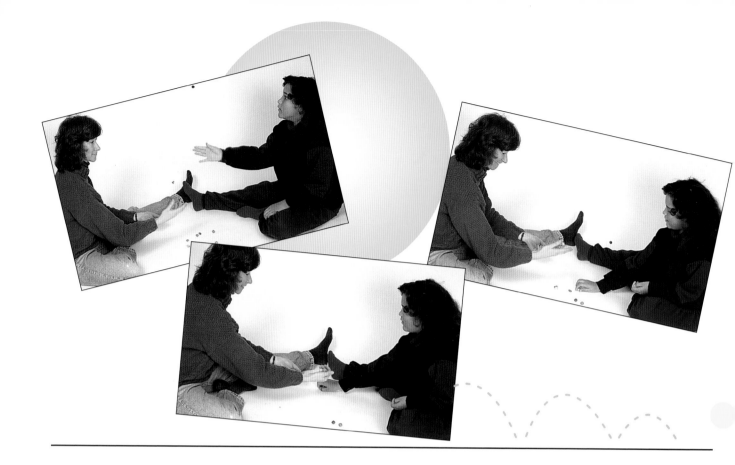

W HAT YOU NEED

- *Old sock without a hole in the toe*
- *Scissors*
- *Shoelace or leather thong, about 12 inches (31 cm) long*
- *11 small, round stones; choose ones that are easy to pick up*

W HAT YOU DO

1. To make a bag in which to keep your pebbles, see the directions on page 57.

2. The following games include some that are easy and others that are more challenging. Experts at these games usually trade their beginner stones in for smaller and more round stones to make the games even more challenging.

Practice Moves:

a. First practice throwing a stone up and catching it with the same hand. Sit on the floor to do this, and concentrate on throwing the stone about 12 inches (31 cm) into the air. When you are very good at catching the stone, try practice move b.

b. Practice throwing a stone up and catching it on the back of your hand without letting it roll off. When you can do that, you're ready for move c.

c. Practice holding five stones in your two hands, throwing them all up at one time, and catching them all on the backs of your two hands held together. Practice until you can catch all five stones without any rolling off.

d. Practice throwing up one stone and picking up another stone while the first stone is in the air, and then catching the first stone without dropping the second one. When you can do that, you're ready to play some games.

Scratches

THIS GAME COMES FROM THE CZECH REPUBLIC, AND IT IS ONE OF THE EARLY GAMES ON WHICH OUR MODERN GAME OF JACKS IS BASED. THE GAME IS STILL PLAYED IN THE CZECH AND SLOVAK REPUBLICS.

1. Play this game with a friend or by yourself for practice. You will need five stones. The first move is called Slugsnail. To play Slugsnail, place four of the stones at the corners of an imaginary square on the floor in front of you, and put the fifth stone on the back of your hand. Keeping the fifth stone on the back of your hand, gather up the four other stones, holding them in the palm of your hand until all four have been picked up. If the stone rolls off the back of your hand, you lose your turn, or, if you are playing by yourself, you must start over.

2. The next part of the game is called Ones. To play Ones, throw down all five stones. Pick up any one and toss it into the air. While it is in the air, you must pick up one other stone and hold it in the palm of your hand while you catch the tossed stone. Put one of these stones into your other hand, and toss the remaining stone while you pick up another stone. Repeat until you have picked up all the stones, one at a time. If you miss or drop a stone, you lose your turn. If you are playing alone, start over if you miss. A variation is for two people to play at the same time with their own stones. They should both start at the same time, and the one who finishes first without a miss wins the round.

3. The rest of the rounds are called Twos, Threes, and Fours. They are played the same as Ones, except that you must toss a stone and then pick up two, three, or four stones at one time.

4. Another move is called Horse. To play Horse, throw all five stones in the air at once and try to catch them on the back of your tossing hand. Then toss into the air any stones that have stayed on your hand, and catch them in the palm of your hand. The winner is the player who catches the most in his or her palm.

5. An advanced move is called Thumber. To play this you'll need an extra stone called the "thumber." Place it in the crotch of your thumb—where your thumb and index finger come together. Hold the thumber in place while you do all the other moves in the game. It must not fall out or be put down with the other stones during the entire time of the game.

Leopard jasper

Knucklebones

THIS GAME COMES FROM THE ISLAND OF MAURITIUS IN THE INDIAN OCEAN.

1. Each player needs ten stones plus a master stone. Each of the ten stones should be about the size of the end of your thumb and easy to pick up. It helps if they are somewhat flat on some surfaces.

2. Hold all ten stones in one hand, toss them, and catch as many as possible on the back of your tossing hand. The ones that you don't catch should be left on the ground. The next play is made with the stones you were able to catch.

3. Toss the stones from the back of your hand into the air, and try to catch them all in the palm of your hand. If you drop any, you lose your turn. If you catch them all, lay those aside in a pile of your winnings.

4. Now repeat steps 2 and 3 using the stones that were dropped in the first step. The winner is the person who picks up all his or her stones in the fewest tosses.

"Sedimental" Journey

*L*ike a restless housekeeper, nature is constantly sweeping up loose bits of dirt and rock, carrying them away, and dropping them as *sediment*. Sediment may be as large as a rock rolling down a mountainside or as small as the dust you find on your windowsill. Nature is a remarkable magician, and can turn all kinds of sediment—pebbles, sand, clay, even the bodies of tiny, dead animals and plants—into rock.

Most sedimentary rock forms under water. In a flooding river, a large rock will get carried just a few feet, while a smaller pebble may bump along for half a mile

ment begins with a thick bed of sand that is changed into *sandstone*. Next, a thin bed of clay is added and hardens into *shale*. This is followed by another bed of sandstone. If you cut through this sedimentary layer cake years later, as rivers or highway builders often do, you can see the beds clearly. You may also see beds that have been tilted by rising magma or folded like an accordion by Earth's moving plates.

Other sedimentary rock is laid down at the bottom of the ocean by the skeletons of tiny floating plants and animals called *plankton*. These creatures may be too small to see, but there are so many of them that when they die their skeletons make thick layers of rock called *limestone*.

A third kind of sedimentary rock is made when the water of a lake or ocean evaporates, leaving behind its minerals. This is how we get table salt for our food: salt water evaporates and leaves the salt called *sodium chloride*.

Intricate crossbeds in Navajo Sandstone. Arches National Park, Utah

before settling and waiting for the next flood. Sand may be swept along for miles, and the mud that turns the river brown may travel all the way to the ocean before it gradually settles to the bottom.

How can all these particles turn into rock? The process may take millions of years as sediment is slowly buried by more sediment piling on top. As the pile gets heavier, the particles near the bottom are squeezed closer and closer together and warmed by the heat of the earth. Groundwater brings new minerals that act like cement to bond the particles together into *sedimentary rock*.

How can you tell if a rock is sedimentary? Often, it is laid down in layers or beds. Imagine that our pile of sedi-

Sometimes a sedimentary rock has no obvious bedding. How can a geologist tell it from an igneous rock? One way is to look at the rock through a microscope. Sedimentary rock grains are smoothed by their travels and surrounded by mineral "cement." Igneous rock grains are jagged and locked together without cement.

You may also wonder: If sedimentary rock usually forms under water, how does it turn into dry land? Remember how active the Earth's crust is? Over million of years, sedimentary rock is pushed upward by rising magma, or the oceans dry up, leaving it behind. In whatever way it becomes dry land, this thin blanket of sedimentary rocks covers most of the Earth's continents.

WHAT YOU NEED

- ½ cup (118 ml) of water
- 2 paper cups
- 2½ tablespoons of Epsom salts (sold at drug stores)
- Spoon
- ½ cup (100 g) of dry sand

MAKING Sandstone

READ HOW SANDSTONE IS FORMED (PAGE 62) AND THEN MAKE SOME OF YOUR OWN. IT WILL TAKE A WEEK OR MORE FOR YOUR SANDSTONE TO HARDEN, BUT THAT'S EONS SHORTER THAN THE TIME IT TAKES REAL SANDSTONE TO FORM!

WHAT YOU DO

1. Put 1½ inches (4 cm) of water in the bottom of one of the paper cups.

2. Dissolve the Epsom salts in the water. Keep stirring until almost all the salt has disappeared. The salt will cement the particles of sand together, just as certain minerals cement sand particles together in real sandstone.

3. Put 1½ inches (4 cm) of sand in the bottom of the other paper cup.

4. Pour the salt mixture into the sand and stir until the sand is completely wet.

5. Let the wet mixture sit undisturbed for about one hour. Then carefully pour off all the water that has risen to the top. You will have to pour off water several times during the first day of the experiment. Keep the paper cup in a place where no one will disturb it for at least one week. Do not cover the cup.

6. When the sandstone has dried completely, tear the paper cup away from it. If you discover that the sides and bottom are still damp, let the sandstone sit undisturbed until it is completely dry. Then, it will feel like real sandstone.

Making a Conglomerate

Like sandstone, a conglomerate consists of particles of minerals cemented together by another mineral. You can make your conglomerate out of pebbles and sand. Decorate the surface with pretty seashells you find on the beach or small rocks and you'll have made an attractive paperweight.

Conglomerate in ancient creek bed. Sevier County, Utah.

- *Water*
- *Paper cup*
- *2½ tablespoons of Epsom salts (sold at drugstores)*
- *Spoon*
- *2 tablespoons of sand*
- *2 tablespoons of gravel*
- *Several seashells or small rocks*

WHAT YOU DO ....

1. Pour 2 inches (5 cm) of water into the paper cup. Add the Epsom salts and stir until dissolved.

2. Add the sand and gravel to the watery mixture, and stir until the sand and gravel are completely wet and mixed. Let the cup sit undisturbed for one hour.

3. After an hour, water will have risen to the top; carefully pour it off. You will have to repeat this step several times during the first day of the experiment as more and more water rises to the top of the sand and gravel.

4. When no more water rises to the top, but the conglomerate is still very wet, push a few seashells or pretty stones into the top of the conglomerate. Half bury them so they'll become part of the conglomerate, but leave part of each sticking out so you can see them.

5. Leave the conglomerate in a place where no one will disturb it for at least one week. It will take a week or longer for the conglomerate to dry and harden.

6. After it is dry, tear the paper cup away from the conglomerate.

Morphed ....

*W*e've learned that rocks can be molten liquid (page 58) and can be formed from sand, clay, and the skeletons of tiny, dead animals (page 62). But there are even more amazing facts in Rocky's Believe-It-or-Not.

Very, very old and cold igneous or sedimentary rocks can be changed by tremendous heat and pressure into different kinds of rocks altogether! Known as *metamorphic rocks* (from the Greek for "change of shape"), these new or "recycled" rocks change into different minerals, shapes, and colors.

How is it possible for solid rocks to be reheated and metamorphosed? This mystery was solved only a few decades ago when geologists found that Earth's crustal plates are always sliding and crunching into each other. All this bashing around can create metamorphic rocks in different ways. When two crustal plates collide, the rocks at the edges of the plates are squeezed and metamorphosed. When one plate is forced under

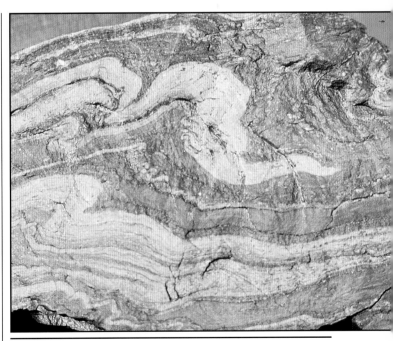

Specimen of wavy folds in schist. Riverside Mountain, California

Hard metamorphic slate that started out as shale, a soft sedimentary rock

another, its rock is plunged into the hot mantle and metamorphosed. When magma rises, it heats and metamorphoses the older rock around it.

Metamorphic rock does not melt, like igneous rock. Instead, it is "baked" under high pressure into a new kind of "bread." Imagine a rock that spends millions of years ten miles (16 km) below the surface! Talk about your hot rocks! There the temperature might be 700°F (370°C) and the pressure 5,000 times as high it is on the surface. It's not surprising that minerals can be "cooked" into new ones, squashed into "layers," and later bent into wavy shapes!

You can get an idea of how this works the next time it snows. Scoop up a handful and make a snowball; press it as tight and hard as you can. The crystals of snow start out light and fluffy, but they get harder and denser because of the heat and pressure of your hands.

Rocks may begin to change even at shallow depths. When sedimentary shale, or mudstone, is baked gently, it becomes smooth, fine-grained *slate*. (Flat beds of slate can be split into shingles for roofs or flagstones for paths. Slate often has fossils in it.)

Deeper down, the shale forms *schist*, which has larger grains and wavy patterns instead of flat ones. These wavy patterns are caused when flat layers are crumpled by pressure, the way you might bend a thin piece of licorice by pushing on both ends.

Rocks called *gneiss* (nice) form under conditions so powerful that the rock becomes almost like plastic and its layers can be bent into S-curves. The dark layers of gneiss are usually *mica*, which form bands between thicker layers of pale or shiny minerals like *quartz* and *feldspar*. Gneiss comes from a German word meaning "sparkle."

Limestone may be metamorphosed into *marble*, which we cut and polish into statues, gravestones, and building blocks. Marble may be almost pure white, or it may have beautiful patterns of green or black minerals such as *olivine* and *serpentine*.

You can see some of the world's most ancient metamorphic rock in the northern United States and Canada—formed more than a billion years ago. Why was so much metamorphic rock made then? Because the Earth was much hotter than it is now, and there was more tectonic activity.

FAUX *Marble*

POLISHED MARBLE
HAS BEEN VALUED FOR
ITS BEAUTY FOR MANY
YEARS. PEOPLE USE
MARBLE FOR TABLE-
TOPS, FLOORS,
MANTLEPIECES,
WINDOWSILLS, AND
MANY OTHER THINGS.
MARBLE IS VERY
EXPENSIVE, BUT YOU
CAN MAKE FAUX
(MEANING "FALSE")
MARBLE THAT LOOKS
AS INTRICATELY
DESIGNED AS THE
REAL THING, WHICH
IS PICTURED BELOW.

WHAT YOU NEED

- *Something to put a marble finish on, such as a light switch plate, wooden box, wooden or plastic picture frame, small bookshelf, or chest of drawers*
- *Fine grit sandpaper*
- *Flat black, gray, or white latex paint*
- *1-inch (2.5 cm) flat paintbrush*
- *3 old pie tins*
- *Flat or semigloss white latex paint (base coat)*
- *2 other colors of flat or semigloss latex paint, one light and one dark: Choose colors that you like and that look good with your project. Pinks, greens, and browns will look the most like real marble.*
- *3 feathers*

1. If the object you plan to marble is wood or metal, sand it all over to make it smooth. If it's plastic, wash it to remove any grease or dirt.

2. Paint the object with the base coat—black or gray or white. Let it dry overnight. Meanwhile, study the picture of marble on page 67 to get an idea of how marble looks.

3. Pour the two colors and the white paint into the three tin pans. Start with the lighter of the two colors. Dip the tip of a feather into the paint, and then tap and drag it across the surface of the object you want to marble. As the feather gets wet it will stick together. When that happens, keep tapping. The tip will swirl around some and make nice patterns. Keep tapping until there is no more paint coming off the feather, and then dip it in the paint again.

4. Next dip the second feather into the darker color, tap and drag it across the surface. It's okay to cross some of the lighter marks. Keep working until you can see nearly equal amounts of the base color and the other two colors.

5. Dip the third feather into the white paint. Make a few long, jagged veins across the piece. These marks will cross over the other colors. They are the characteristic vein marks that make marble look like marble.

6. Let the piece dry overnight before using it.

METAMORPHIC Rocks

*L*IKE METAMORPHIC ROCKS, THESE BAR-SHAPED COOKIES ARE FORMED PARTLY BY PRESSURE AND HEAT. YOU'LL BE ABLE TO SEE THE LAYERS OR STRATA IF YOU LOOK AT THE CUT EDGES AFTER YOU SLICE THEM INTO SMALL SQUARES. TRY CHANGING THE INGREDIENTS OR REPEATING THE LAYERS TO MAKE YOUR OWN SPECIAL METAMORPHIC ROCKS. THIS IS ONE KIND OF ROCK YOU CAN SAFELY CHEW ON WITHOUT BREAKING YOUR TEETH!

WHAT YOU NEED

- *Oven*
- *Glass or aluminum baking dish, about 9 by 6 by 2 inches (23 by 15 by 5 cm)*
- *Measuring cup*
- *¼ cup (60 g) of butter or margarine*
- *Hot pad*
- *1½ cups (200 g) of cookie and/or graham cracker crumbs: To make your own, put cookie or graham cracker pieces between two large sheets of waxed paper and crush them with a rolling pin.*
- *6 ounces (250 g) of sweetened condensed milk*
- *3½ ounces (100 g) of flaked coconut—or crushed wheat cereal or chopped raisins*
- *4 ounces (110 g) of shelled and chopped nuts— or unsalted sunflower seed kernels*
- *4 ounces (110 g) of semisweet chocolate chips—or try butterscotch, mint chocolate, or milk chocolate*
- *3½ ounces (100 g) of granola*
- *Waxed paper*
- *Dull knife, such as a butter knife*
- *Spatula*

WHAT YOU DO

1. Preheat the oven to 325°F (163°C) for a glass pan or 350°F (176°C) for an aluminum pan.

2. Place the butter or margarine in the pan. **Ask an adult to help you put the pan in the oven** for a few minutes to melt the butter.

3. Use the hot pad to remove the pan from the oven. Sprinkle the cookie or graham cracker crumbs on top of the melted butter. Here we used half of each type of crumbs.

4. Pour the condensed milk evenly over the crumbs, trying not to disturb them.

5. Sprinkle on a layer of each of the following ingredients in this order:

    -shredded coconut, crushed wheat cereal, or raisins

    -chopped nuts

    -chocolate chips

    -granola

6. Place a piece of waxed paper on top of the mixture and press down all over. Either use the palm of your hand or the bottom of the measuring cup.

7. Peel off the waxed paper. Use the hot pad when you put the pan back in the oven. Bake the cookies for 25 to 30 minutes until the top layer is lightly browned.

8. Let the pan of cookies sit out for 15 minutes and then refrigerate for one hour.

9. When the cookies are cool, slice them into bars with the knife. Use the spatula to lift the bars out of the pan. Yum! If you have any left to store, keep them loosely covered in the refrigerator.

Weather Wear

Left: Good example of the effect of weather on rock. Rainbow Bridge National Monument, Utah

Below: Dramatic example of erosion. Polk County, Tennessee

Have you ever studied an old tombstone in a cemetery? Often the rock has worn down so much you can hardly read the names and dates.

This is a good example of *weathering*—the wearing down of rock by the weather and other natural forces. If you see how much a tombstone changes outdoors after only 100 years, you may understand how whole mountains can disappear over millions of years.

Nature uses many tricks to break down rock. The first is to create small and large cracks in rock. Cracks may form as rock cools or as heavy rock on top of it erodes away. These cracks are enlarged when water gets inside them, then freezes and expands. Salt crystals may also expand in the cracks.

Plants are powerful weathering agents. You've probably seen how tree roots can break up sidewalks. Roots can do the same thing to layers of rock, wedging apart even large boulders and opening them to more weathering. If a tree blows over in a storm, it exposes more rock and pries others loose.

Another powerful weathering agent is fire, which can cause rocks to shatter. You may think that natural fires are rare, but remember that geologic change takes a long time. In almost every area with grasses or trees, lightning causes many wildfires over the course of millions of years.

There are also many kinds of *chemical weathering*. Rainwater carries many kinds of chemicals that can dissolve minerals from rock. As these minerals are removed, the rock weakens and weathers more rapidly.

Weathering is a very important part of the rock cycle. It helps to break old rocks and even mountains into the sediment that forms new sedimentary rock. Even more important for us, some of this sediment produces the soil that allows us to grow crops, grasses, and trees.

Erosion Experiment

Spend a few minutes poking around in the garage or basement and you're sure to find all you need to set up an erosion table. Then get your scientific mind in gear as you devise experiments to show the effects of rocks, plants, and contouring on the way water erodes land.

What You Need

- *Something to use as a container: A paint roller pan is perfect, or try a dishpan, long wallpaper pan, baby bathtub, long plastic windowsill planter or planter trays, or old lasagna pan.*
- *Piece of wood, 2 by 4 inches (5 by 10 cm) or a brick (if you are NOT using a paint roller pan)*
- *Bucket of soil or sand; sandy soil works best*
- *Trowel*
- *Plastic knife, putty knife, or a flat stick for shaping the soil*
- *Large nail*
- *2 paper cups*
- *Water*
- *Rocks, small blocks of wood, small clumps of moss, twigs from short-needled evergreen trees, lichens, pebbles, model railroad trees—or any other objects that you can use to imitate plant growth*

1. If you are not using a paint roller pan, place the brick or piece of wood under one end of your container so that it will have a slope and water can drain away from the landform you will build.

2. Build a hillside at the high end of the container. Fill the entire end of the container, and build the hill at least 5 inches (13 cm) high.

3. Use the nail to poke four or five holes in the bottom of one of the paper cups. Space the holes evenly so that the bottom of the cup looks like a watering can spout. Fill the other paper cup with water.

4. For your first experiment, hold the holey paper cup about 12 inches (30 cm) over the hill, and pour water into it from the other cup. Move your hand around so that rain falls evenly on the hilltop. Watch to see what happens to the hill as rain falls on it. Make some notes in your notebook or draw a picture of the before and after.

5. Let the water drain to the low end of the container, then carefully pour only the water out. The soil should stay at the other end of the container. Now put the container back on its brick or piece of wood, and rebuild the hill. This time, add some rocks to the hill. Create another rain shower, and watch what happens to the hill. Make notes or drawings.

6. Keep emptying water and rebuilding the hill each time you change the experiment. Try planting trees made of moss or evergreen twigs; try contouring the hillside in different ways, much as farmers do when they plant crops on hillsides. Each time, build the hill as much as possible as it was built at first, and note what happens when it rains. Try placing some small blocks of wood (houses) on the hillside in different places, and watch what happens to them when it rains. What does this experiment show about the effect of plants, rocks, and different kinds of contouring on erosion?

From Rock Into Soil

A soft coating of soil covers most of Earth's continents like a blanket. But even on the best farmlands, this blanket is only a few feet thick. Without it, Earth would look like a hard ball of rock—no trees or bushes, and—most likely—no people.

The process of making soil begins with weathering, which breaks rock into small particles. Rocks weather fastest where it's rainy and warm. That's why a desert has only a few inches of soil or none at all. Antarctica is a dry, frozen land with practically no soil.

But soil is more than just little pieces of rock. It's softened by a mixture of decayed plants and animals known as organic matter, or *humus*. This humus is needed to hold water and nourish the roots of trees, crops, and other plants.

Soil also has living ingredients—countless numbers of ants and worms, gophers and moles, and billions of tiny organisms too small to see. The activities of these creatures help to break down leaves and branches into more soil.

One way to understand soil better is to cut a deep trench in the ground. First you'll see the darkest soil with most of the humus, which geologists call the *A-horizon*. This zone is full of life, and the soil looks and smells alive. Next you'll find the *B-horizon*, where the soil is rougher and there is little life or organic matter. Below that is the C-horizon, which is mostly broken and decayed bedrock mixed with some clay. Under the *C-horizon* is rock—all the way to the center of the Earth.

The recipe for making good soil is complex. First you take plenty of rainwater and chemicals to soften up the rock. Then you add the decaying bodies of dead plants and animals to make humus. Finally, you let the earthworms, gophers, and beetles dig around and mix the soil so the bits of rock break down faster.

Even for the best "cook," working in the best "kitchen" with plenty of rain and mild temperature, it may take more than 200 years to make enough soil to grow a forest. In dry climates, even thousands of years aren't enough to form fertile soil.

That's why it's so important to protect our topsoil from washing away or eroding. We need good soil to grow our food, and it takes a long time to make more.

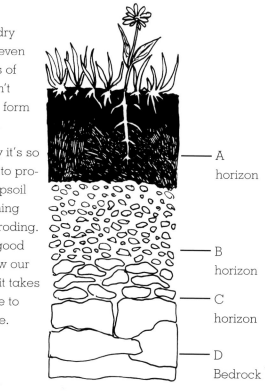

A horizon

B horizon

C horizon

D Bedrock

Don't Forget Clay

■ One of the most important minerals found in soil—or anywhere else—is clay. Clay makes up about a third of all sediments on Earth. We use it to make so many things—bricks, pottery, tile, china, and cement, to name a few.

■ The most useful clay mineral is called *kaolin*; this is what we make pottery and china from. Another is *bauxite*, a tropical clay where most of our aluminum comes from. Another common clay is *montmorillonite*, mostly made from volcanic ash.

■ All clays are made of sheets of minerals that may slide apart when wet. If you're taking a rainy day hike and the trail has lots of clay in it, watch out: wet clay can be as slick as ice!

■ Where does clay come from? Like all other sediments, it comes from the breakdown of rocks. Clay minerals are formed when rainwater causes rocks containing feldspars to weather and fall apart. Some of the chemicals in feldspar wash away, and clay is what's left behind.

MOSS + ROCK GARDEN

DELICATE MOSSES IN VARIOUS SHADES OF GREEN CAN BE REPLANTED TO GROW OVER BEAUTIFUL ROCKS TO MAKE AN INTERESTING TABLETOP GARDEN. HUNT FOR MOSSES IN DAMP PLACES, BUT DON'T OVERLOOK CREVICES IN ROCK WALLS, CRACKS IN SIDEWALKS, AND THE BARK OF OLD, ROTTING TREES.

WHAT YOU NEED

- Collection of fresh mosses and lichens
- Shallow dish, such as a plant saucer or a dish garden planter
- 2 to 3 handfuls of pebbles
- Several trowels of rich garden soil or well-rotted compost
- 10 to 12 medium-sized rocks

WHAT YOU DO

1. Collect mosses and lichens in wooded areas or parks or damp areas of a yard. There are many kinds of mosses and lichens. Some are fuzzy and green and look like velvet. Others look like tiny ferns. Lichens, which are really two plants that grow together—one an algae and the other a kind of fungus—often look like curly, leathery, gray-green skins attached to tree bark or rocks. Look around rotting tree stumps or on rocks near streams or springs. As you collect, keep the plants in plastic bags with a little water in the bag to keep the plants damp.

2. Place a layer of pebbles in the bottom of the planter or dish. Then add a layer of soil. Arrange rocks over the soil and tuck the mosses in among the rocks. Finish by watering the garden.

3. It is important to water the moss garden often—every other day or even every day, depending on the dryness of the room. Mosses and lichens need dampness to live. They don't mind being cold (in fact, they do better in cool places than in hot, dry places) as long as they are wet. Try misting your garden every day with cool water, in addition to watering it.

Snowflake obsidian

HUNTING FOR Clay

You can buy clay in a craft-supply store, but you can find your own if you know what to look for and where to look. The nice thing about finding your own clay is that the pieces you make from it will have come from your own special place on the earth and will remind you of that place whenever you look at or use them.

WHAT **Y**OU **N**EED

- *Trowel*
- *2 buckets*
- *Sieve or strainer: To make your own, nail four pieces of 1-by-2-inch (2.5 by 5 cm) lumber to form a square, and then use a staple gun to attach a square of hardware cloth to the wooden frame.*
- *Piece of window screening as big as the sieve or slightly larger*
- *Old T-shirt*
- *Piece of plywood at least 3 by 3 feet (91 by 91 cm)*

WHAT **Y**OU **D**O

1. The best place to find clay is the banks of a creek. Walk in the shallow parts of the creek and watch for places, low on the bank, where the soil looks slick or slippery. Often clay is bluish gray or rusty orange. It will almost always be a different color from the regular soil nearby. The best test is to feel the clay. It should stick together and feel slippery when it's wet. Try rolling a chunk of it into a worm. If the worm holds together without completely crumbling, you have found clay.

2. Dig the clay, trying not to get ordinary soil or sand mixed in with it. Use a bucket to carry the clay.

3. Now you must clean the clay. Fill the bucket three-quarters full with clay; then add water almost to the top of the bucket. Use your hands to break up lumps of clay. The object is to mix the clay and water thoroughly. Take out any large rocks or twigs.

4. After the clay and water are mixed, you will have a bucket of what is called *slip*. Place the sieve over the second bucket, and pour the slip through. The sieve will catch any large or medium-sized rocks or twigs or other material.

5. Wash out the first bucket and the sieve. Spread the screen on the bottom of the sieve and place the sieve and screen on top of the bucket.

6. Pour the slip through the screen/sieve. This time smaller rocks and debris will be caught by the screen. The slip should be fairly smooth and clean by now. Some people stop after this step. If your slip feels silky smooth, go on to step 9. If it feels gritty, go to steps 7 and 8 first.

7. To get the slip even cleaner, you can sieve it through a cloth. Wash out the empty bucket and put it inside the old T-shirt so that a single thickness of cloth is stretched over the opening of the bucket.

8. Slowly pour the slip through the cloth. The T-shirt will droop and stretch, so pour slowly. If it droops too much, pull it tighter. You may have to add some water to the slip so that it will go through the T-shirt. It may take awhile for the slip to seep through the shirt. If the shirt becomes clogged, take it off the bucket and rinse it.

9. Let the clean slip sit in the bucket overnight. You'll see water rising to the top after a couple of hours. Pour or scoop the water off as it rises. Continue scooping off water until you get as much off as you can.

10. Pour the thick slip onto the piece of plywood so that even more water can evaporate. Put the plywood out in the sun, but be sure to cover it or bring it inside if it rains! Check the slip often. As soon as it is thick enough for you to shape into a ball, roll or scrape it off the plywood, and store it in a plastic bag. Let it sit for a couple of weeks and it will be nicer to work with. Be sure to keep the bag sealed.

A Primitive KILN

DID YOU KNOW THAT YOU CAN BAKE
OR FIRE CLAY IN YOUR OWN BACKYARD
USING A PROCESS THAT IS THOUSANDS
OF YEARS OLD? WITH HELP FROM AN
ADULT, YOU CAN BUILD AND USE A
SIMPLE PRIMITIVE KILN THAT WILL
TURN YOUR CLAY OBJECTS INTO HARD,
PERMANENT PIECES WITH A BEAUTIFUL
SMOKEY GRAY OR BLACK COLOR.

WHAT YOU NEED

- *Hammer*
- *Awl or large nail*
- *Metal garbage can with a lid*
- *Large flat-head screwdriver*
- *Bricks or flat stones to put under the kiln*
- *Bucket of water*
- *Enough dry sawdust to fill the garbage can*
- *Old newspapers*
- *Matches*
- *3 small wads of wet clay*
- *Hot pad*
- *Medium-sized rock to weight down the can lid*

WHAT YOU DO

1. Using the hammer and nail or awl, punch a row of
three holes on each of four sides of the can. **1** Use
the screwdriver to enlarge the holes until they are at
least ½ inch (1.5 cm) across.

2. Place the bricks or stones on the ground for the kiln to stand on. It's best to put the kiln on ground that has no grass growing on it and to clear away any dry leaves or other things that could easily catch fire. Keep the bucket of water nearby to use in case of an emergency.

3. Put 4 inches (10 cm) of sawdust in the bottom of the kiln.

4. Carefully place the first layer of clay pieces you want to fire, leaving 2 to 3 inches (5 to 8 cm) between each piece and 4 inches (10 cm) between the pieces and the kiln walls. If you are firing bowls or pots, fill the insides of them with sawdust, too.

5. Cover the layer of clay pieces with 3 to 4 inches (8 to 10 cm) of sawdust, and place another layer of clay you want to fire.

6. Keep layering your clay pieces until you reach the top 6 inches (15 cm) of the can. Then add 2 inches (5 cm) of sawdust and finish off with twists of news-paper. To make a twist of newspaper, first pleat half a sheet of newspaper. Then twist the folded paper, starting at the center. **2**

7. Place the twists of newspaper side by side to fill the top layer of the kiln.

8. Put three small wads of wet clay equal distances apart on the rim of the can. These will hold the lid up enough to vent the fire and let it breathe.

9. **Ask an adult to light the newspaper.** Once the twists have caught fire, rest the lid on the clay wads to cover the kiln.

10. Check the fire often until it is going smoothly. Make sure the sawdust lights after the newspaper twists burn out. If you see smoke coming from the can, the fire is lit. If the sawdust stops burning, add more newspaper twists and **have an adult relight them.** You should not see flames after the newspapers burn out, but you should continue to see smoke. Put a rock on the lid to hold it in place.

11. What you are aiming for is a slow, even smoldering that burns from top to bottom. Sometimes it takes several tries to get the kiln started. There is very little danger of a fire starting from a metal can kiln. Keep the cover on when you aren't around, and you can leave it for several hours and even overnight. Place a sign warning people not to touch it.

12. After 24 hours, when smoke is no longer coming from the kiln, remove the rock and lift off the lid. Be sure to use a hot pad for this operation. The sawdust should be black and the top layer of clay pieces should be visible. Let the pieces cool (may take several more hours), then carefully remove them. Brush off any remaining sawdust.

13. Pieces fired in a primitive kiln are not waterproof. They are stronger than they were before being fired, but they are still rather easily broken, so handle them with care. Rub the pieces with a soft rag to bring out the black, gray, or white shine.

1

2

Clay Beads

Beads made of clay and fired in a primitive kiln have a dark smokey gray, mysterious look. They make beautiful necklaces or decorations on books. If you leave out the holes, you can use them for game stones.

What You Need

- Two large handfuls of clay
- 12-inch (31 cm) piece of dental floss
- 2 old corks
- Round toothpicks or uncooked spaghetti

1. Before making beads (or anything else out of clay), you need to wedge the clay in order to get rid of air bubbles that could cause it to break when it is fired. Wedge the clay by slamming it down on a tabletop, then pounding and lifting it, turning it, and pounding it again. Continue pounding-lifting-turning the clay for ten minutes.

2. To see if the clay is thoroughly wedged, try this: Tie each end of the dental floss to a cork. Hold the floss taut by pulling on the corks, and use it to cut through the lump of clay. Examine the flat sides where the slice was made: they should be smooth. If they are, slam them together and go on to the next step. If there are any holes or cracks, continue wedging for a few more minutes, then test again.

3. Take a small pinch of clay and roll it into a ball or a cylinder. If you want a square-sided bead, flatten each side and each end by gently tapping it on the table. Use a toothpick to draw designs on the bead.

4. Holding the bead gently between your thumb and index finger, poke a toothpick or a piece of uncooked spaghetti through the bead until it sticks out the other end. Leave the toothpick or spaghetti in there. It will burn away when the bead is fired, leaving a clean hole.

5. Place the finished beads in a single layer—not touching each other—on cookie sheets or old pie tins or on pieces of wood where they won't be disturbed. Let the beads dry for several days. To check for dryness, hold one of the biggest beads against your cheek. It should not feel cool. If it feels cool, put it back and let the beads dry for a few more days.

6. You are now ready to fire your beads. See the instructions on page 79 for making and using a primitive kiln.

Earth CRAYONS

Keep your eyes open for beautiful colors of soil and clay when you go for a walk. When you find some, scoop up a trowel or two, and store it in a plastic bag. When you have a good collection of several different colors of browns, reds, yellows, and oranges, you can make earth crayons.

WHAT YOU NEED

For each color:
- *Sifter*
- *1 cup (145 g) of sifted soil*
- *Heavy cloth, such as an old dish towel (optional)*
- *Hammer (optional)*
- *2-quart-size (2 l) saucepan*
- *Piece of beeswax, about ½ by 2 by 2 inches (1.2 by 5 by 5 cm); sold at many craft-supply stores*

- *Piece of paraffin the same size as the beeswax; sold at grocery stores*
- *Clean empty tin can, 16-ounce-size (454 g) or larger*
- *Hot pad*
- *4 teaspoons of turpentine*
- *Old wooden or stainless steel spoon; do not use sterling silver as it conducts heat*
- *Several sections of old newspaper*

WHAT YOU DO

1. Sift the soil or clay to get out all pebbles and pieces of debris. The finer the particles, the better. If the soil is lumpy, break it up with your fingers first. For the finest soil, pour the soil into a heavy cloth and pound it with a hammer.

2. Fill the saucepan with 2 inches (5 cm) of water.

3. **Ask an adult to help you with the rest of this project.** Place the beeswax and the paraffin in the tin can and place the tin can in the pot of water. Carefully put the pot on a stove and bring the water to a boil. When the water begins to boil, turn down the heat so that it simmers but does not boil hard.

4. After a few minutes the wax and paraffin will melt. When this happens, carefully add the turpentine. Stir it, and then slowly add the cup of sifted soil. Stir until the soil is completely mixed into the wax and paraffin.

5. Use the spoon to scoop out the waxy soil. As it is scooped, it should be drained slightly against the side of the can. This mushy, waxy soil is VERY HOT. Be extremely careful when handling it. The mush should be placed in a couple of small mounds on several thicknesses of newspaper. Let the mush cool some, until you can see the liquid wax at the edges of the mound turning white and hard. While the mush is cooling, tap it lightly with the back of the spoon to make a patty, like a mudpie, so that it will cool faster.

6. After a few minutes the mush will be cool enough to handle, but still warm enough to be soft. **Ask your adult friend to test the mush for coolness.** When it is cool enough to handle (usually about ten minutes), scrape it into a pile and begin to form your crayons. Here's how to form them: Push the mush into a snake shape about 3 inches (8 cm) long. With your thumb on one side and your other fingers on the other side, pinch the top of the snake into a long wedge shape. Next, lift the snake (the bottom should be flat, the top pointy), and turn it so that the bottom becomes a side. Flatten and shape this side just like you did the first one. Finally, turn the snake to its third side and flatten and shape. You should now have a crayon that has three long, flat sides. Flatten the ends, and put it aside to cool completely while you form the other crayons.

7. To make other colors, clean out the tin can (or use another can) and repeat steps 1 through 4.

8. These crayons work best on rough, dull-finish paper, such as charcoal or construction paper. Experiment to see what works best with your crayons. Each type of soil will give a slightly different kind of crayon. If the soil that you use has mica dust in it, your crayons will have glitter dust in them! Because your colors will be limited to the colors that soil comes in, try combining them with cut or torn colored papers when you make pictures and designs. If you draw a picture of your backyard or the woods down the street, you'll have the satisfaction of showing the true colors of the rocks and soil in your neighborhood.

Rocks That Grow

Although lots of people have a favorite rock they carry in their pocket like a pampered pet, rocks aren't alive (oh, you knew that!). But did you know that some rocks can "grow"?

The most well-known type of growing rock is limestone, which grows into huge, thick *coral reefs*. The "coral" part, of course, is really a small, wormy animal that looks like a miniature sea anemone.

What does a wormy little animal have to do with rock, and why isn't it swept away by the ocean waves? This animal discovered the art of building construction way before we humans did. Corals are clever enough to secrete the mineral calcium carbonate to glue themselves together in sturdy underwater apartments. Some of these coral condos are called staghorn coral because they look like antlers. Others are called brain coral because they look like you-know-what, often several feet in diameter. These fancy structures provide shelter for colorful fish, crustaceans, and algae.

You may think that a tiny animal can't make all that much rock. The secret is... lots of tiny animals! Millions of little corals working for thousands of years can secrete a lot of limestone. If you have any doubts, check out the Great Barrier Reef, off the east coast of Australia. It's more than 1,200 miles (1,920 km) long—and all built by coral.

Corals sometimes live along the coast, and sometimes on the top of huge ocean islands called *atolls*. These atolls are the carcasses of giant volcanoes that are sinking slowly back into Earth's hot mantle. The coral animals need to be near sunlight, so they keep growing upward (and adding limestone) as fast as the island sinks. When they die, their limestone skeletons crumble in the waves, sink to the bottom, and are covered by more skeletons. This growing pile of sediment gradually becomes sedimentary rock (see page 62). Atolls may be a mile high—all underwater and all made by coral.

Another kind of rock that grows is *dripstone*, or cave rock—which is also limestone. When groundwater seeps through the limestone around a cave, it picks up the limestone mineral, calcium carbonate. If the water seeps through the roof of a cave and evaporates, it leaves behind its mineral load, a drop at a time. This mineral gradually builds into needle-shaped *stalactites* that hang from the ceiling like icicles. If the water drips to the floor, it builds up *stalagmites*—blunt, upside-down icicles.

This doesn't happen overnight; it may take dozens or even hundreds of years to grow an inch of dripstone. Sometimes stalactites and stalagmites join, forming thick *columns* from roof to floor. The dripstone formations in Carlsbad Caverns in New Mexico are so spectacular that visitors come to see them from all over the world.

Left: Coral reefs in the Virgin Islands

Top: Stalagmites and stalactites in the "Kings Palace" in Carlsbad Caverns National Park in New Mexico

Right: Other cave formations in Carlsbad Caverns

Limestone CAVE

This simple experiment lets you watch a process that takes many, many years in real life.

What You Need

- Scissors
- Clear plastic bottle, such as a small bottled-water container
- Piece of aluminum foil
- Large nail
- Glass bottle or jar with an opening larger than that of the plastic bottle
- 5 cups (725 g) of sand
- Spoon or trowel
- 1 cup (200 g) of granulated sugar or sugar cubes
- 1 cup (236.6 ml) of warm water

5. Put a 2-inch (5 cm) layer of damp sand in the plastic bottle. Press it down so there are no air spaces.

6. Put a 1-inch (2.5 cm) layer of sugar or sugar cubes on top of the sand. Be sure it is pressed against the side of the bottle and filled in solidly. The sugar represents limestone under the ground.

7. Put another 2- or 3-inch (5 or 8 cm) layer of sand on top of the sugar. Press out all spaces. You should be able to clearly see three layers.

8. Pour ½ cup (118.3 ml) of warm water on top of the top layer of sand. Wait until it drains down, and then pour the other ½ cup (118.3 ml) of water. Watch what happens to the limestone (the sugar) after two or three hours. What has caused the caves that you see? What does this show you about how caves form underground?

WHAT YOU DO

1. Cut off the bottom half of the plastic bottle. Remove the cap.

2. Fit the piece of aluminum foil over the opening of the plastic bottle. Use the nail to punch a few small holes in the foil.

3. Place the plastic bottle inside the opening of the larger glass bottle.

Garden MARKERS

BRIGHTLY PAINTED STONES MAKE CHEERFUL GARDEN MARKERS. NO MORE WONDERING WHAT YOU PLANTED WHEN ALL THOSE LOOK-ALIKE SEEDLINGS COME UP!

WHAT YOU NEED

- *Smooth potato-sized rocks, the flatter, the better*
- *Old pie pan*
- *Acrylic paints*
- *Paintbrushes*
- *Container for water*

WHAT YOU DO

1. Wash the rocks and let them dry completely.

2. Paint a picture of a different plant on each rock.

3. Let the paint dry completely before placing the markers in your garden.

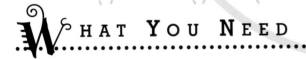

Rock Jewelry

A ROCK NECKLACE OR RING IS A WONDERFUL WAY TO SHOW OFF SOME OF THE MOST INTERESTING OR BEAUTIFUL ROCKS IN YOUR COLLECTION. IT TAKES PRACTICE TO USE NEEDLE NOSED PLIERS, AND AT FIRST THE ROCKS MIGHT KEEP JUMPING OUT OF THEIR WIRE CAGES. BUT WITH A LITTLE PATIENCE, YOU'LL SOON BE DESIGNING YOUR OWN ROCK JEWELRY.

What You Need

- *Assortment of interesting small rocks*
- *Roll of soft jewelry wire, gold- or silver-colored (sold in craft-supply stores)*
- *Wire cutters*
- *Needle nosed pliers*
- *Thin leather thong or heavy cotton string, 12 inches (31 cm) long*

What You Do

To make a necklace

1. Place the rocks on a table in the order you would like them to hang from the necklace.

2. You must attach a wire to each rock. Use the wire cutters to cut 12 inches (31 cm) of wire. Place the rock on the wire near the middle of its length. Hold the rock down while you wrap one end of the wire

over the rock as in figure **1**. Now bring the other end of the wire over the rock, crossing over the first end of the wire. **2**

3. Turn the rock and wire over and repeat step 2. **3**

4. Twist the wire a few times as you pull the wire ends up toward one end of the rock. **4**

5. Use the needle nosed pliers to help twist one of the ends of wire into a small loop. **5**

6. Wrap the wire ends a few times to tighten the neck of the loop, then snip off both wires as close as possible to the loop neck. Use the needle nosed pliers to flatten the pointy ends of wire and to push them against the neck of the loop. **6**

7. Wrap all the other rocks with wire in the same way.

8. Slip the first rock by its wire loop onto the thong or string and place it where you want it to be. Carefully tie a knot to hold the rock loop in place. Twist the loop so that the front of the rock is facing front when the necklace is on the table.

9. Tie all the other rocks onto the necklace the same way.

10. Try on the necklace, tying it in back so that it hangs the way you want it to.

To make a ring

1. Use the wire cutters to cut two pieces of wire, each about 15 inches (38 cm) long.

2. Lay the wires side by side on the table and place a rock on top of both wires, midway along their lengths. **7**

3. Wrap both wires at once over the rock. Twist the wires. **8**

4. Now wrap the two wires on the left side all the way around the rock in the other direction from the first wrap, and meet the other wires at the same twisting spot. Twist all four wires again. **9**

5. Form a finger-sized loop with the two longer wires, twisting them a couple of times under the rock to hold the loop. **10**

6. Use the wire cutters to snip off all four wire ends as close as possible to the twist under the rock. Use the needle nosed pliers to flatten the short wire points and to press them into the twist.

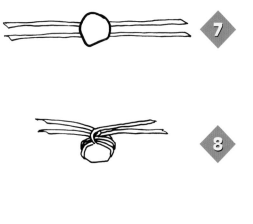

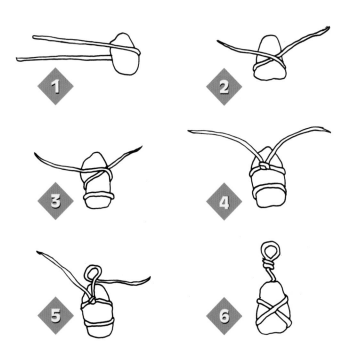

Fossils: Signs of Ancient Life

*i*magine this: an insect becomes caught in the sticky resin of a pine tree. The tree blows down in a storm and is covered by a mud slide. Millions of years later the insect is found perfectly preserved in the resin, which has turned to a stone called *amber*.

And this: a dinosaur walks across a field, its huge feet sinking into soft sand. A dry wind blows and the footprints fill with dust. Later the prints are buried in sand, which hardens into sandstone. Millions of years later the sandstone erodes and exposes the footprint.

And this: a young man is fishing on a lake shore in Africa three million years ago. A sudden noise frightens him and he falls into the lake and drowns. A storm covers him with mud, so that his bones are preserved and hardened into stone.

In all these stories, the insect, the dinosaur footprint, and the early human have become *fossils*. *Paleontologists*, the scientists who study fossils, roam the world finding teeth, bones, leaves, or footprints that have turned to rock.

Some fossils look like their modern relatives, such as oysters, clams, possums, sharks, and horseshoe crabs. Others, such as flying reptiles and piglike, cud-chewing beasts, look more like extraterrestrial creatures from a bad dream! But every fossil gives us clues about what—or who— lived on the earth millions of years ago.

In a few places, paleontologists have found whole, large animals or plants. For example, a few woolly mammoths have been found perfectly preserved in permafrost in Siberia. Near Los Angeles, California, whole saber-toothed tigers and other large animals were fossilized when they fell into a big tar pit. And in the desert

of Arizona there are whole trees that have been turned to stone, or *petrified*.

Unfortunately, these fantastic signs of ancient life are very rare. It takes very special conditions to make a fossil, and most animals vanish without a trace.

Think of an ancient fish that dies. Chances are another fish would quickly eat it, or it would decay. The bones would probably fall apart and dissolve in water. Even if it were preserved, a flood might come along and wash it away or break it to bits.

For the fish to become a fossil, it has to be quickly buried in mud or shale. Then it has to be protected against erosion for many thousands of years while all the atoms of its bones are replaced by minerals. Finally it becomes a rock (a fossil) within a rock (a sedimentary rock).

This is why most fossils are formed in the ocean. On land, dead organisms are exposed to weathering by rain and wind—the forces that wear away rocks. In the ocean, dying organisms sink to the bottom where they are protected from the weather. Most ocean critters are tiny, floating plants or animals called *plankton* which have limestone shells; these shells easily harden into tiny limestone fossils.

We can learn a lot about the ancient world from fossils. For instance, if we find warm-water plankton all over the world in a certain time, we can be pretty sure the climate was warm when they lived. If we find cold-loving plankton, we can bet that this plankton lived in an ice age, when glaciers covered much of the earth.

Man pointing to dinosaur tracks east of Moenkopi. Coconino County, Arizona

Fossil CAST

FOSSILS ARE INTERESTING RECORDS OF THE PAST, BUT THEY ARE ALSO BEAUTIFUL TO LOOK AT. IN THIS PROJECT YOU CAN SPEED UP TIME AND MAKE A FOSSIL MOLD OR CAST IN JUST A FEW HOURS. YOUR FOSSIL CAST WILL HAVE THE SAME DETAILS AND DELICATE PATTERNS THAT A REAL FOSSIL HAS.

WHAT YOU NEED

- *Chunk of plasticene (modeling) clay the size of your fist*
- *Dull table knife*
- *2 paper cups; bottom should be 2 to 3 inches (5 to 7 cm) in diameter*
- *A well-formed seashell, small bone, or seedpod*
- *About ½ cup (63 g) of plaster of Paris (sold at hardware and hobby- or craft-supply stores)*
- *¼ cup (59 ml) of water*
- *Spoon*

1. Make a ball of clay and flatten it until it's about 1 inch (2.54 cm) thick and smooth on top. Trim the circle of clay with the knife until it fits into the bottom of the cup.

2. Slide the clay into the cup, flat side up. Carefully press the object you want to fossilize into the clay until it's half buried. Then carefully lift the object out of the clay. You will be able to see an impression or print of the object.

3. Pour ½ cup (63 g) of plaster of Paris into the other paper cup. Add ¼ cup (59 ml) of water to the plaster of Paris and stir until the mixture is smooth. Leave it alone for five minutes.

4. After five minutes, the plaster of Paris mixture will have thickened. Pour it into the other paper cup right on top of the clay. Let this sit for an hour without touching it.

5. After an hour, the plaster of Paris should be almost completely hard. It will feel cool, and you will still be able to make marks in it, so be careful with the next step. Carefully tear away the sides of the paper cup and remove the clay and plaster. Holding the clay part with one hand and the plaster part with the other hand, gently separate them.

6. Clean off the clay part and put it away. You can use it for other projects. Use the knife to carefully trim away any rough edges from the plaster fossil cast. Smooth out the edges, then let it dry for a day or two until it no longer feels cool when you hold it against your cheek. Be sure to let it dry slowly and not in an oven or in the sun. Drying it too quickly could cause it to crack.

Seed Cast Medallions

Using the process for making a fossil cast (see opposite page), you can make casts of small leaves, seedpods, dried flowers, bones, shells, and even feathers. A few extra steps transform these fossil casts into medallions to use as holiday decorations, window ornaments, or wall hangings.

What You Need

- Chunk of plasticene (modeling) clay the size of your fist
- Scissors
- 2 paper cups; bottom should be 2 to 3 inches (5 to 7 cm) in diameter
- Small, hard objects to cast, such as seedpods, leathery dried leaves, shells, bones, feathers
- ¼ cup (59 ml) of water
- Food coloring
- Spoon
- ½ cup (63 g) of plaster of Paris (sold at hardware and hobby- or craft-supply stores)
- Large nail
- Small container to hold glue
- Waterproof white craft glue
- Paintbrush
- Thin string or ribbon

WHAT YOU DO

1. Make a ball of clay and flatten it on both sides so that it is smooth, round, and about 1/2 inch (1.5 cm) thick.

2. Cut a ring out of the paper cup, about 1/2 inch (1.5 cm) wide.

3. Press the ring into the flattened clay. Be sure the paper cuts slightly into the clay as this ring will form a container for the plaster of Paris.

4. Press the object that you want to cast into the clay so that it's at least half buried. If it is a thin object, such as a leaf or feather, use the flat bottom of a cup or glass to press.

5. Carefully remove the pressed object. Be sure to get out any crumbs or broken pieces.

6. Pour ¼ cup (59 ml) water into the second paper cup. Add a few drops of food coloring to the water and mix it in. Then pour ½ cup (63 g) plaster of Paris into the water. Stir quickly, and let the mixture sit for five minutes undisturbed.

7. After five minutes, the plaster of Paris mix will be slightly thickened. Stir it again, then pour a layer about ¼ inch (1 cm) thick into the paper ring on top of the clay. Let it sit undisturbed for one hour. Don't worry if some plaster of Paris leaks out from under the paper ring; just add a little more to the ring to replace what leaked out. The plaster will quickly thicken and stop leaking.

8. After one hour, carefully tear the paper ring away from the medallion and lift the medallion from the clay. The plaster will still be cool and wet, but it will be firm, and you will be able to see all the fine details of the fossil cast. Carefully poke a hole in the top of the medallion with the nail. Let the medallion dry for a day or two until it no longer feels cool when you hold it to your cheek.

9. When the medallion is completely dry, paint all surfaces with white glue. The glue will dry clear and will protect the medallion against water and dampness.

10. Put string through the hole in the top of the medallion and hang it in a window, on a holiday tree, or on a wall.

THE Big Time LINE

IT'S HARD TO UNDERSTAND THE ENORMOUS NUMBERS WE MUST USE WHEN WE TALK ABOUT THE AGE OF THE EARTH. THIS PROJECT WILL LET YOU SEE A MODEL OF THOSE BILLIONS OF YEARS.

WHAT YOU NEED

- *5 sheets of construction paper, each a different color*
- *Scissors*
- *Glue stick or white craft glue*
- *Markers or crayons*
- *2 empty toilet paper rolls or an empty paper towel roll*
- *Transparent tape*
- *Piece of ribbon, 2 feet (61 cm) long*

WHAT YOU DO

1. Fold each of the pieces of colored paper in half lengthwise. Press hard on the fold to make a good crease. **1**

2. Cut each piece of paper along the crease. Glue the two halves of each piece of paper together end to

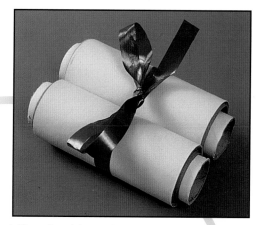

end. You should now have five long pieces of colored paper. Each piece represents 1 billion years. **2**

3. Now glue all five sheets end to end. You will now have one very long piece of paper.

4. Lay the piece of paper out on the floor. Begin marking at the left end of the strip of paper. Halfway across the first color (where the two pieces of paper are glued together) draw the Earth, for this is approximately when the earth was born—four and a half billion years ago.

5. Next move to the next color, and draw a fossil halfway across this color (again, in the place where the two sheets are glued together), for this is the time of the oldest fossils that have been found— three and a half billion years ago.

6. Leave the next two colors blank. These are the two billion years during which only a few organisms seem to have existed. If you want, you can draw a few more fossils in these colors, but only draw a few, and space them out widely.

7. Halfway across the last color draw some fish, for this is the time when abundant life seems to have started, around 500 million years ago.

8. Now things get crowded. Right after the fish, draw some reptiles and amphibians (snakes, frogs, and salamanders, for example). Keep them in a top-to-bottom row, because there are more creatures to draw in the few inches of space that you have left!

9. After the reptiles and amphibians, draw some mammals, such as wooly mammoths, tigers, or horses.

Right after the mammals, draw some dinosaurs, for they lived and died out between 200 and 100 million years ago.

10. Finally, at the very end of the time line, draw some humans, for it was not until the past 50 to 75 thousand years that humans have lived on the earth—as far as we know. Fifty thousand years sounds like a long time until you see how small that section of the time line is compared to four and a half billion years!

11. Tape a paper roller to each end of the time line to make a scroll. **3**

12. Roll the scroll from both ends toward the middle. **4**

13. Tie your scroll with the piece of ribbon. Find a big space on the floor to unroll it so that you get to see the whole long line at once. What a lot of years!

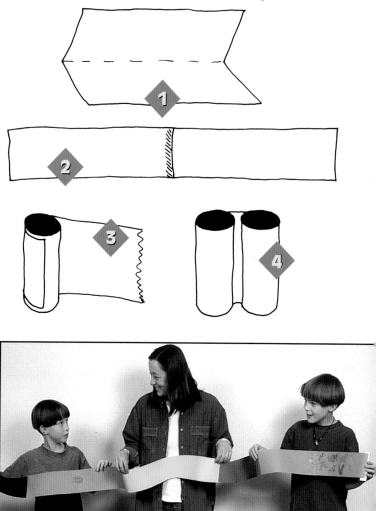

The Geologic Time Scale

For most of human history, people thought Earth was created only a few thousand years ago. Now we know that our story is a whole lot longer—and it's a story written in the rocks. But for a long time, nobody could "read" the rocks: they all looked, well, like rocks!

One of the first people to learn to read the rock record was William Smith, an engineer helping dig canals in England two centuries ago. As the work crew dug through sedimentary rock full of fossils, Smith could see that the rocks were arranged in layers, or *strata*. Some of these strata were paper-thin; others were several yards thick. After a while he realized that each stratum had to be younger than the ones below it and older than the ones above it. This makes sense—unless

someone is running around sliding young rocks underneath older ones!

The next thing Smith realized was that strata were piled up in the same order from one region to the next. He could tell partly by the way the rocks looked and partly because each layer had its own special mix of fossil creatures. Smith became so familiar with these fossils that he could tell at a glance which layer a particular piece of rock came from. Little by little, geologists around the world found that rocks with the same fossil "fingerprints" are the same age no matter where they are found.

About a century after Smith's work came another big discovery: that many rocks contain tiny amounts of *radioactive elements*. These elements, such as uranium, decay at a steady rate into "daughter" elements, such as lead. Knowing the rate of decay and the amount of parent and daughter material, geologists have a "radioactive clock" for calculating a rock's age. This is how we know that Earth is about 4.6 billion years old.

Using these tools, geologists have been able to draw a chart of history called the *geological time scale*. This scale, which took a century and a half to construct, is

| Paleozoic Era ~ 345 million years | Mesozoic Era ~160 million years | Cenozoic Era ~ 65 million years |

divided into four large units of time called eras—the *Precambrian, Paleozoic, Mesozoic,* and *Cenozoic, Eras*—and each era is many millions of years long.

The first three eras are named after the Greek words for modern life, middle life, and ancient life. Each era is divided into smaller divisions called periods. These periods were named after the places where the rocks were first found: The *Devonian Period* was named for rocks found in Devon, England; *Permian* after the region of Perm in Russia; *Jurassic* for the Jura Mountains of Europe; and so on. The most recent (*Tertiary*) period is divided into shorter *epochs.*

Far left: Part of star dunes. Northeastern part of Namid Desert, South West Africa

Left: Dunes in northwestern Namid Desert in South West Africa. The dune in the background is about 300 feet (92 m) high.

Above: U-shaped valley in Glacier National Park, Montana

Right: Yellowstone Canyon. Yellowstone National Park, Wyoming

The Precambrian Era is the longest part of the time scale: 80 to 85 percent of the entire age of the earth. This is everything that happened on earth from 4.5 billion years ago until 570 million years ago. Yet we know much less about that time. It was so long ago that most of the rocks—along with the evidence of what happened—have been weathered and eroded, or "morphed" into new rocks.

Chapter 3

Minerals, Minerals, Everywhere

We find many reasons to study minerals. One is to enjoy their beauty. Another is to understand their structure.

A third reason is that so many of the things we use in modern life come from minerals, including all the metals and thousands of chemicals.

For example, iron is found in minerals such as *magnetite* and *hematite*. Aluminum is mined from the mineral *bauxite*. Titanium, used to strengthen the metal of the space shuttle, is refined from the minerals *ilmenite* and *rutile*.

Nonmetal minerals are equally important. How would our food taste without salt, evaporated from seawater? How would we plaster our walls without *gypsum*, another

evaporite? How would we make glass without quartz? Or pottery without clay? Or lime without limestone?

The problem, of course, is to find places where there is plenty of the mineral we want. And that's what geologists spend a lot of their time doing.

In this chapter, we'll learn that rocks are made of minerals, and minerals are made of crystals, and crystals are made of atoms. And we'll also begin to see why so many minerals are so important to our lives.

Crumpled layers in evaporite salt deposits near the Dead Sea in Jordan

Building Blocks of Rocks

You know that a house is often built out of boards, nails, and bricks, but do you know what rocks are built out of? The building blocks of rocks are *minerals*. A rock like limestone is built mostly of a mineral called *calcite*; rocks like granite or gneiss are built out of several minerals.

Now comes the hard question: What is a mineral? The easy answer is that a mineral is a form of *matter*, like water or air or wood. But what do the *insides* of a mineral look like? If we had super-vision and could peer through any kind of matter, we'd see that a mineral is made of huge numbers of *atoms*. An atom is so small that if we enlarged one 100 million times, it would still be only about the size of a pea!

Until about a century ago, scientists thought atoms were the smallest possible particles. Now we know that each atom has a large *nucleus* at the center and tiny *electrons* that vibrate around the nucleus.

Halite

These electrons are like the nails of a house; they hold matter together. Here's how. Some atoms have "extra" electrons and some have "missing" electrons. When an atom of an element with extra electrons, such as sodium, meets an atom of an element that needs an electron, such as chlorine, the atoms join together by sharing an electron and becoming a *molecule* of sodium chloride. Sodium chloride is also known as the mineral *halite*, and when you find it in the grocery stores, it's called table salt.

When atoms are sharing electrons like this they are "charged up" with energy and are called *ions* (EYE-ons, from the Greek word "go"). The attraction between some ions can be as strong as...rock! These strong attractions, or *bonds*, between ions are what make a mineral so hard and rigid—just like a house held together with strong nails.

Some ions have just one kind of matter, some have more. When atoms of carbon and oxygen bond together, they make an ion called *carbonate*; atoms of silicon and oxygen make an ion called *silicate*. These big ions can share electrons to make minerals just like smaller ions can. Carbonate ions can combine with calcium ions to form calcium carbonate, or *calcite*, the mineral of limestone. The chalk your teacher uses to write on a blackboard is a soft kind of calcite.

There are other common minerals in rocks—*oxides* (oxygen combined with other ions), carbonates, *sulfides* (sulfur combined with other ions), *sulfates* (sulfur-oxygen ions combined with other ions), and *phosphates* (phosphorus-oxygen ions combined with other ions).

That's too many minerals to keep straight, you say? How can anyone possibly understand rocks? Don't worry: most rocks only have a few different kinds of mineral building blocks, and more than half of the Earth's rocky crust is made up of silicate minerals. Whew! The commonest mineral of all is a silicate called *feldspar*, a name that comes from two Swedish words, feld (field) and spar (mineral). Swedish farmers gave it that name because their fields had so many feldspar rocks they could hardly plow through them.

Another really common mineral, *quartz*, has only silicon and oxygen ions. Most of the beach sand in the world is little specks of quartz. Feldspar and quartz together make up three-fourths of the Earth's crust. So if you look at the big picture, most rocks really aren't all that complicated.

Rock Candy

One type of crystal that you can grow not only looks pretty, but tastes good, too! If you have lots of patience, you can make rock candy out of sugar and water.

What You Need

- 1 cup (200 g) of granulated sugar
- ½ cup (118 ml) of water
- Cooking pot
- Food coloring (optional)
- 2 heat-proof glass jars or small bowls
- Dull table knife

What You Do

1. Put 1 cup (200 g) of sugar into the pot. Add ½ cup (118 ml) of water, but do not stir the mixture.

2. **Ask an adult to help you put the pot on the stove over medium high heat.** Let the mixture come to a boil and let it boil for one minute without stirring.

3. If you want colored candy, add a few drops of food coloring as the mixture boils.

4. **Ask an adult to help you carefully pour the mixture into one or two glass jars or small bowls.**

5. Let the containers sit undisturbed for two weeks. Gradually crystals will begin to form. Check the candy every day. When a crust forms on the surface, tap it with a dull knife to break the crust so the water can continue to evaporate. Otherwise, don't move or disturb the containers.

6. When the crystals are as big as you want them to be, break the candy from the container with a table knife, and prepare yourself for a sweet and tasty treat. Yum!

Crystals and Their Shapes

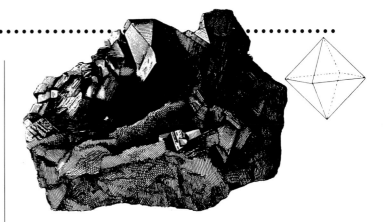

One way to understand minerals is to think about the way they're put together—their *structure*, or shape.

Think about water. When water is a liquid or a gas, the molecules can zoom around in any direction. The molecules don't have any structure. But when water temperature drops below 32°F (0°C), the molecules slow down and freeze into a rigid geometric shape, like eggs in a carton. This rigid shape is a *crystal structure*. Every time ice freezes, anywhere in the world, it always makes the same crystal structure. One way to describe a mineral is: a solid material that always has the same crystal structure.

Quartz cluster

If we could see into a crystal, we would see that all the ions are locked in little clusters called *unit cells*. The unit cell of the mineral halite (which we also call table salt) has four chloride ions and four sodium ions. Each unit cell is so small that in a single grain of salt there are more than 5 million million million of them, all arranged in regular patterns like bricks in a wall.

If we take a large chunk of halite and tap at it carefully with a hammer, we can break it into a squared-off piece that looks just like a life-sized ice cube. And here's the really amazing part: The shape of a large cube of halite is a life-sized version of the shape of its little, invisible unit cells! This is true for all minerals: the shape of a large piece is a gigantic version of its microscopic unit cells. (Pretty cool, eh?)

One more thing: knowing a mineral's crystal structure helps to explain why it breaks in a certain way. Minerals always break in the direction where the ionic bonds between unit cells are weakest. For example, the unit cells of mica are arranged in flat sheets, like playing cards. The bonds between the sheets are weak, and you can easily pull them apart with a fingernail. In other minerals, like quartz, the unit cells may be locked together in all directions—and they won't break at all.

To get a good idea of how beautiful some crystal patterns are, take a magnifying glass outside after it snows and look at a snowflake. When water freezes, its hydrogen and oxygen ions lock into many different hexagonal (six-sided) shapes. And it's true what they say about snow flakes: hexagons can be arranged in so many different ways that the crystal pattern of every flake is different!

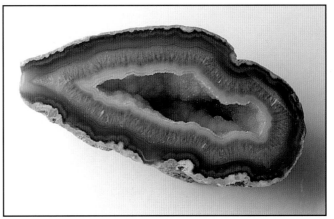

Geode crystals growing inside holes in rocks

How Crystals Grow: The Birth and Growth of Quartz

Most crystals are born in magma, that fiery liquid rock many miles below Earth's surface. There is so much heat in magma that atoms and molecules zing back and forth like angry bees. They have too much energy to hook up and form solid matter. But if the magma rises near the Earth's surface and starts to cool, all those particles lose energy, slow down, and look for partners.

The hot molecules that make quartz are called *silica*. The atoms of silica always lock into a shape called a *tetrahedron*, which means foursided figure. A silica tetrahedron has one silicon ion sitting right in the middle of four oxygen ions, all of them sharing

Smoky quartz

electrons. That's why the chemical symbol for silica is written SiO_4—one silicon, four oxygens.

When magma cools, each silica tetrahedron starts to huddle up with another tetrahedron, then another, and another, up and down and sideways. Many millions of them all lock together in a growing crystal of solid quartz. If the magma cools too fast, like volcanic lava that is thrown onto the earth, the tetrahedra don't have time to get organized into crystals and instead they form a dark glass called *obsidian*.

The silica tetrahedra of quartz hold each other so tightly in so many directions that they are almost impossible to break apart. That's why quartz is so tough, and why we find quartz sand on beaches all over the world. All the other rock minerals have broken apart or dissolved in the rain, leaving the tough little crystals of quartz all by themselves.

Most quartz crystals don't grow big enough to see.

Rutilated quartz

That's because in a magma, lots of chemicals are trying to grow all at once, some faster than others, and they get in each other's way. But sometimes, in a protected pocket of rock where a crystal has plenty of room and no competition, it might grow to several inches or more. A really perfect quartz gemstone would look like a clear, six-sided cigar with hexagonal pyramids at each end; this is called *rock crystal*.

Sometimes atoms of other elements in the magma get mixed up with the silicon and oxygen. This can change the color of quartz to yellow, pink, brown, or even black. Violet quartz, which has tiny amounts of manganese or iron, is called *amethyst*, a semiprecious gem. When tiny air bubbles make the quartz cloudy, it's called *milky quartz*. Other gems of quartz are *agate* (with colored bands), *flint* (gray), *jasper* (red), and *opal* (quartz plus water). The best thing to do with these minerals is to make them into jewelry!

Quartz cluster

THE ATOMS IN A CRYSTAL ARRANGE THEMSELVES IN AN ORDERLY WAY. YOU CAN WATCH HOW THIS HAPPENS IN THIS EXPERIMENT. PRETEND THAT THE MARBLES ARE THE ATOMS IN THE CRYSTAL.

CRYSTAL Theory EXPERIMENT

WHAT YOU NEED

- *Between 40 and 100 marbles, all the same size*
- *Several round, shallow containers, such as large jar lids, plastic tub lids, and cake pans; the more marbles you have, the bigger the container you can use; if you have only 40 marbles, use jar lids and round plastic tub lids.*
- *Notebook and pencil*

WHAT YOU DO

1. Place a few marbles in a single layer in your smallest container. Notice whether or not they form a pattern all by themselves.

2. Continue adding marbles until no more will fit in a single layer. Now look for a pattern. Draw one if you see one.

3. Repeat steps 1 and 2 in a larger container. Notice any patterns and draw them, too. Compare them to the patterns you found in the smaller container.

4. Repeat steps 1 and 2 in the largest container that you have. What happens? Try taking out a few marbles and stirring the others around so that the patterns are broken up. Now put the marbles back in until no more will fit in a single layer. What happens? Draw any patterns that you see. Compare the patterns in the biggest container with those from the other containers. What do you think would happen if you had twice as many marbles and a really big container?

5. A real crystal isn't flat, so an actual crystal pattern is not in a single layer and is deep as well as wide. This experiment does give you an idea of what happens in a crystal when atoms arrange themselves.

Growing CRYSTALS

You've probably come across directions for growing a crystal garden. Unfortunately, most crystal gardens don't look anything like gardens. They are fairly messy looking—not at all decorative like a small moss or cactus garden. So we aren't calling this project a garden at all. What it is, though, is a very interesting experiment that lets you get a good look at the fascinating patterns of crystals as they form.

What You Need

- Minerals to grow into crystals:
    Epsom salts (sold at drugstores)
    table salt
    alum (sold at many drugstores and craft stores)
- Water
- Measuring cup
- Small pot
- Wooden spoon
- Food coloring (optional)
- Several small glass custard dishes or bowls
- Glass canning jars—one for each kind of crystal you want to grow
- Handful of clean rocks or pebbles
- String
- Scissors
- Pencils or thin sticks—one for each kind of crystal you want to grow
- Notebook and pencil

WHAT YOU DO

1. First decide which kind of crystals you want to grow. Then make a solution of that mineral and water. Here are the "recipes" using the different minerals.

Epsom salts

Put 1 cup (200 g) of Epsom salts into ½ cup (118. 3 ml) of water in a pot. **Ask an adult to help you bring the mixture to a boil on the stove.** Stir the mixture to help dissolve the Epsom salts. What you are making is a saturated solution, which means that there is almost too much Epsom salts to stay in solution in the water.

Table salt

Mix ¾ cup (177.4 ml) of water and ½ cup (100 g) of salt in warm water. Stir until the salt dissolves. Again, this is a saturated solution, so some salt crystals may sink to the bottom and refuse to go into solution. That's okay.

Alum

Mix ¼ cup (50 g) of alum into 1 cup (236.6 ml) of hot water. Stir to dissolve the alum.

If you want to grow colored crystals, add a few drops of food coloring to each mixture now.

2. Now you have some choices to make. One way to grow crystals is simply to pour the solution over a few clean pebbles in the bottom of a glass bowl. Pour enough so that the solution reaches the top of the pebbles. Another way is to pour the solution into a glass jar and hang a string from a pencil so that the string dips into the solution. You might want to try both ways of growing crystals; pour half your solution in a bowl and half in a jar.

3. Here's your next choice. Crystals grow differently in a hot place than they do in a cool place. It might be interesting to put one container in the refrigerator and another in a warmer place, such as near (but not on) a heater, or in a sunny spot. If you are growing more than one kind of crystal, be sure to label each container by sitting it on top of a piece of paper with its name written on the paper.

4. Leave the crystal solution undisturbed for several hours. It's important not to move the container while crystals are forming. After a few hours, check to see what has happened. This would be a good time to make a drawing of whatever crystals have formed and to note the time, the temperature of the location, and any other facts that might be important.

5. Check the containers the next day and see what has happened. Make more notes and drawings. You may be able to come to some conclusions, such as what difference the temperature of the location makes to the way crystals grow. You can also note differences in the way crystals grow on rocks versus the way they grow on a string.

6. When some good-size crystals have formed, try scooping them out with a spoon. Many crystals will hold their wonderful shape as long as you don't get them wet. If you get a lot of pretty crystals, you could arrange them in a small glass bowl for a different kind of "crystal garden."

Paper Crystal Models

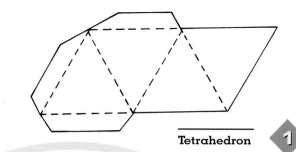

Tetrahedron ◀ 1

THE FORMS OF CRYSTALS
HAVE FASCINATED PEOPLE
SINCE THE TIME OF THE
ANCIENT GREEKS.
HUNDREDS OF YEARS AGO,
SCIENTISTS BEGAN TO
DEVELOP THE STUDY OF
MATHEMATICS BY INVESTI-
GATING THE FORMS OF
CRYSTALS. THE FOUR
CRYSTAL FORMS IN THIS
PROJECT APPEAR IN MANY
MINERALS. YOU CAN HANG
THESE CRYSTALS IN A WIN-
DOW OR USE THEM FOR
HOLIDAY DECORATIONS.

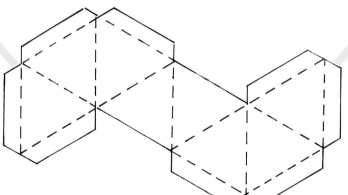

Octahedron ◀ 2

WHAT YOU NEED

- *Several sheets of tracing paper*
- *Sharp pencil*
- *Pencil sharpener*
- *Colored construction paper or origami paper*
- *Transparent tape*
- *Scissors*
- *Paper clip*
- *Ruler*
- *White craft glue*
- *Glitter (optional)*
- *Thread*
- *Sewing needle*

WHAT YOU DO

1. Enlarge the patterns on a copier by 200%. Then trace them carefully.

2. Turn over the sheet of tracing paper and color the entire back of the traced figure with pencil. Be sure to color the back of all lines.

3. Place the tracing paper, right side up, on top of the back of the colored paper. You want the pencil side to be against the back of the colored paper. Lay both sheets of paper on a hard surface, such as a tabletop. You may want to tape the tracing paper to the colored paper to hold it securely.

4. Trace over all the lines of the pattern, pressing hard with a freshly sharpened pencil. Your lines must be sharp and clean. Trace broken lines over the dotted lines, and solid lines over the solid lines.

5. When you have finished tracing, remove the tracing paper. You should be able to see the design in light lines. Use those lines as a guide to cut along all solid lines. Do not cut any dotted lines. Those are the fold lines.

6. When you have cut out the figure, use the ruler and paper clip to crease all the dotted lines. Creasing them will make them easier to fold. Using the ruler will insure that the lines are straight.

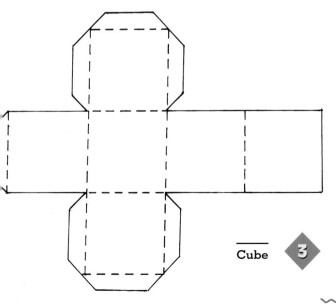

Cube 3

7. Fold all the dotted lines that you have creased. All folds should be made with the wrong side of the paper facing up. As you fold, you will easily see how to glue the tabs to form the figure.

8. After the figure is folded, put a few drops of glue on each tab. Now fold the figure, and when you come to a tab, press it against the side or tab that it is next to. On some of the forms, you may have to hold the tab for a few minutes while the glue sets. (The folds should be hidden inside the paper forms.) If you are making the dodecahedron, trace the pattern, and cut two pieces of paper at the same time, so that you have two identical patterns. When you fold and glue each of the two sides, you will see that they form bowl-like shapes with pointy edges. Put glue on the edge tabs of one of the bowls and fit the other into the jagged shapes to form one crystal.

9. If you want to decorate your crystals, use glue and glitter.

10. Thread the needle, knot the thread, and push it in and out of one point on each crystal. Hang the crystal from the thread.

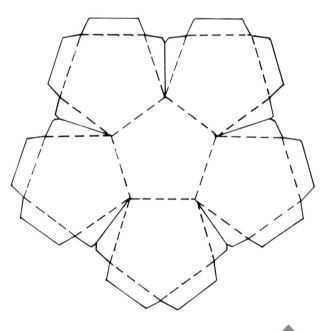

Dodecahedron 4

A Mineralogist: The Sherlock Holmes of Geology

You've just used a rock hammer to carefully chisel out a golf ball-sized chunk of mineral from the side of a cliff. Its color and shape appeal to you, but what kind of mineral is it? There are hundreds of different minerals…how can anyone know what each one is?

Mineralogists are scientific detectives who use many clues to identify minerals. One of the best clues is *hardness*. You may think all minerals are hard—hard as a rock, right? Some are, some aren't. Quartz is too hard to scratch with a pocketknife, but gypsum is soft enough to scratch with your fingernail. Talc is the softest mineral known (it makes the talcum powder you may put on after a bath) and you can scrape it into powder with your fingernail.

Mineralogists use the *Mohs' scale*, shown on page 114, to rank minerals, from 1 (talc) to 10 (diamond). Any mineral on the scale will scratch any mineral below it. Topaz (#8) scratches quartz (#7); quartz scratches feldspar (#6); and so on.

What makes a mineral hard? Think about crystal structure and the strength of the bonds between atoms. The stronger the bonds between atoms in all directions, the harder the mineral.

Okay, some of you are now asking: If diamond is the hardest mineral, how can you cut a diamond to make diamond jewelry? Here's the answer: With another diamond!

Another clue to identify a mineral is its *cleavage*. Think of a butcher with a meat cleaver: he whacks a chunk of meat and makes a clean, flat cut. If you break a mineral by dropping it on a rock or breaking it with a hammer, it will cleave along flat surfaces, or planes. Each mineral has cleavage planes that are always at the same angle from one another. By measuring that angle a mineralogist has an important clue. (See "Crystals and Their Shapes," page 105.)

You might think the *color* of a mineral is a dead give-

Fluorite

away. It is, for a few minerals, such as blue azurite, green malachite, yellow sulfur, or red cinnabar. But usually minerals occur in several colors. Fluorite may be colorless, yellow, brown, pink, greenish, blue, violet, or almost black. How can that be? It's because color is not something solid that's part of the mineral; it's really just light-wave information gathered by your eyes. The "color" of these light waves gives you information about how they've been bent and reflected as they pass through the crystal structure of a mineral. If there is a tiny change in crystal structure, the light is bent differently and you see a different color. For example, the mineral corundum is made of aluminum oxide and usually has a white or grayish color. But when just a few atoms of chromium replace a few atoms of aluminum, it becomes blood red and we call it a ruby. Or when you add a dash of iron and titanium, corundum becomes a deep blue and we call it a sapphire. (And pay a lot of money for it!)

Because color isn't very reliable, mineralogists also use another clue called *streak*. A streak is a thin swipe of powder you can make by scraping a mineral against a white porcelain plate. If the mineral is really hard, you can scrape the mineral with a file to get some powder onto the streak plate. A streak may surprise you: The mineral magnetite has a blackish color, but its streak is always red! And the streak of the yellowish mineral pyrite is always greenish black.

Luster is another clue. Luster is what the surface looks like: metallic—a polished metal surface; vitreous—bright as glass; resinous—sticky as the sap on a pine tree; pearly—pretty as a pearl; and greasy—like a film of oil. Two minerals may have the same color but different lusters.

Still another clue is *density*—how heavy the rock feels. If you hold the same-size chunk of a light mineral like quartz in one hand and a heavy mineral like magnetite in the other, you can easily tell the difference. In heavy

Mohs' Scale

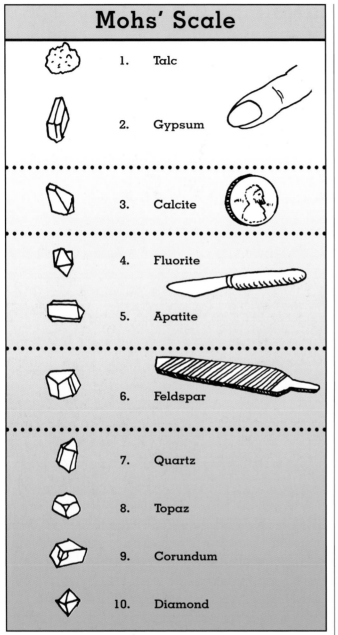

	#	Mineral
	1.	Talc
	2.	Gypsum
	3.	Calcite
	4.	Fluorite
	5.	Apatite
	6.	Feldspar
	7.	Quartz
	8.	Topaz
	9.	Corundum
	10.	Diamond

minerals (gold is one of the heaviest), the atoms are packed tightly together.

So, about that chunk of mineral you're holding. If you were a mineralogist, you'd put all these clues together to decide what this mineral is. Does it have a whitish streak, a vitreous luster, a density of 4, and hardness of 9? Then you're probably holding a chunk of corundum. Does it have a yellow streak, a metallic luster, a density of 17, and a hardness of 3? Then get on down to the bank: That's a nugget of gold in your hand!

What a Gem!

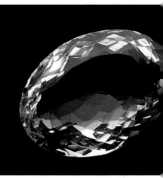

Aquam

We all know what a *gem* is—the shiny, glittering stone found in jewelry. But what makes a gem a gem?

If you've read this far in the book, you probably know that a gem is a mineral. But not all minerals have what it takes to be a star: perfect crystals, beautiful colors, and sparkling lights. If there are any bubbles, cracks, or cavities—forget it! That mineral hasn't got what it takes! A gem is also rare.

A crystal of quartz, even a perfect one, wouldn't interest

Opals

a picky gem collector. There is just too much quartz in the world.

One of the rarest—and most valuable—gems is *diamond*, which is made when pure carbon is "cooked" and crushed for a long time, more than 90 miles (144 km) below the Earth's surface. When carbon is cooked at lower temperatures and pressures, it just becomes graphite—the soft, black "lead" used in pencils. The pressure has to be really high to pack the atoms of carbon into the perfectly hard mold of diamond, the hardest substance known.

Now you're wondering—if diamonds come from so deep in the Earth, how do they get to the surface? No one knows for sure. But most diamonds are found in long volcanic channels called *kimberlite pipes*, named after the city of Kimberley, in South Africa. Very hot magma was probably pushed upward through these pipes by explosive gases—like the engine of a Saturn 5 rocket turned upside down. But the magma stopped and cooled (with its load of diamonds) before reaching the surface. The largest known diamond, which was found in a kimberlite pipe, weighed almost a pound and a half (681 g)!

Beryl (named for the rare metal beryllium) is usually a pale grayish or greenish mineral that may grow to enormous size: one crystal has been found that was 30 feet (9.2 m) long and weighed over 25 tons (27 t)! Even more interesting to us is the beryl that has just the right mix-

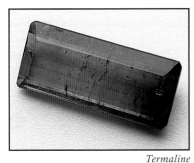
Termaline

ture of atoms to turn it bright green. This is the gem we call *emerald*, one of the most valuable on earth.

Corundum is a simple mineral containing just aluminum and oxygen. Like beryl, it may be a drab gray to yellow or colorless. But add a dash of the metal chromium and you've got yourself a *ruby!* Or a touch of iron and titanium and look out! It's a *sapphire!* Even ordinary corundum is so hard (9 on the Mohs scale) it is used to make emery paper, a very rough abrasive.

Opal is a class of gems that is just like quartz except that it doesn't have a crystal structure; it is more like glass. It may be pale pearly blue or pink to nearly black; the gem collector's favorite is milky white opal.

Sapphires

Topaz

A mineral needs one more thing to be a precious stone: it has to be really hard. Can you think why? Most gems are formed inside igneous or metamorphic rocks. The rocks gradually weather, fall apart, and dissolve, except for the hard quartz—and gems. Many gems are swept downhill by rain into rivers, where they tumble along with pebbles and rocks— which would chip or break them if they weren't really hard. At the end of their journey they often settle in piles of sand,

Ruby zoicite

Peridot

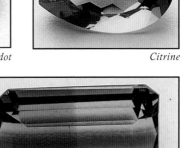
Citrine

pebbles, and rocks along the mouth or banks of a river. There they can be found by a hardworking (and very lucky!) rock hound— who could be you!

Amesite

Gems from a river bank look very different by the time they wind up in jewelry stores. About 400 years ago, people discovered that you can make a gem look even more brilliant and colorful by making small, flat cuts called *facets* in the surface. Jewelers figured out the exact angles of these facets so that the light that enters a gem is trapped for a while, bouncing back and forth inside the gem and increasing its brilliance.

Amethyst

Treasure Boxes

These beautiful boxes look as if they were made of gold, silver, and precious gems, but in fact they cost very little to make. They make wonderful gifts, or you can use them to hold your personal treasures.

What You Need

- Variety of small, interesting boxes, such as egg crates, small wooden cheese boxes, or small cardboard boxes; don't use boxes with waxy, shiny surfaces
- Gold, silver, or copper acrylic paint (sold in art- or craft- supply stores)
- Paintbrush
- Aluminum foil
- White craft glue that dries hard and clear
- Small bowl
- Food coloring
- Spoon
- Scissors

116

1. Begin by painting the boxes with metallic paint. Paint all the surfaces, and let them dry.

2. While the boxes are drying, make your gems. On a table or countertop, spread out a piece of smooth, unwrinkled aluminum foil, about 12 inches (31 cm) long.

3. Pour a small amount of glue into the bowl and add a few drops of food coloring. Stir with the spoon to thoroughly mix the coloring. You can either use pure colors or mix colors, such as red and blue to make violet.

4. Drop blobs of colored glue onto the aluminum foil, keeping them at least 1 inch (2.5 cm) away from each other on all edges. The blobs will spread out a little, depending on how much food coloring you have added. If they spread until they are completely flat, mix more glue into the colored glue to thicken them. The blobs should form rounded ovals and circles on the aluminum foil.

5. When you finish with one color, wash out the bowl and spoon and make another color. Leave one batch white so that it will dry clear and you will have some "diamonds."

6. Let the gems dry for several days. You can tell they are dry because they will become glassy. At first the blobs will look like colored glue. As they dry, a clear colored, glasslike ring will form around the outside of each gem. The more the glue dries, the bigger the glassy ring will become. When the gems are completely dry, they will look like diamonds, rubies, topazes, or other gems.

7. After the gems are dry, cut them out with scissors into round, oval, or faceted shapes.

8. Glue the gems to your painted boxes. Fill the boxes with treasures!

Rock Mobile

A mobile made of rocks sounds strange! Rocks are heavy, and objects in a mobile seem to float. But pretty rocks can become airborne; twisting on the ends of thin pieces of thread, they can nicely decorate a window.

W HAT YOU NEED

- *Collection of small, pretty rocks*
- *Twig that has at least one branching fork*
- *Roll of silver- or gold-colored jeweler's wire (sold at craft- supply stores)*
- *Wire cutters*
- *Needle nosed pliers*
- *Spool of sturdy thread*
- *Scissors*
- *Craft glue*
- *Large metal paper clip*

1. Select the rocks that you want to use. Place them on a table next to the twig and see if they look too big or too small.

2. You must attach a wire to each rock. To do this, begin by cutting 12 inches (31 cm) of wire. Place the rock on the wire near the middle of its length.

3. Hold the rock down while you wrap one end of the wire over the rock. **1 (Figures 1 through 6 are the same as for "Rock Jewelry" on page 92.)**

4. Now bring the other end of the wire over the rock, crossing over the first end of the wire. **2**

5. Turn the rock and wire over and repeat steps 3 and 4. **3**

6. Twist the wire a few times as you pull the wire ends up toward one end of the rock. **4**

7. Use the needle nosed pliers to help twist one of the ends of wire into a small loop. **5**

8. Wrap the wire ends a few times to tighten the neck of the loop; then snip off both wires as close as possible to the loop neck. Use the needle nosed pliers to flatten the pointy ends of wire and to push them against the neck of the loop. **6**

9. Wrap all the other rocks with wire in the same way.

10. Tie a piece of thread about 10 inches (25 cm) long to the loop of each rock. Tie the other end of each thread to the twig in an arrangement that you like.

11. Dip your thumb and index finger of one hand in glue, and rub glue along the length of each piece of thread. Use the glue to stick the loose ends of thread to the main strings for a neater look.

12. Bend the paper clip into a large hook. Wrap one end of it around the middle of the twig, as in figure **7**. Use the other hooked end to hang the mobile.

Chapter 4

How We Use Rocks and Minerals

You're sitting at the kitchen table, doing your homework or reading a newspaper. Ah, there's no place like home. But let's take a look around. Yikes! Better put on a hard hat! Your house is full of rocks and minerals!

Your family's stove and refrigerator and all the other metal appliances in your home are made from ores such as iron, chromite, and nickel. Those ceramic tile countertops, the linoleum floor covering, the dishes in your cupboard, even the paper you're reading contain clay minerals. There's quartz in your television, stereo, and watch. The "lead" in your pencil is made of a mineral called graphite.

Everything plastic and all the synthetic fabrics in your house—including, probably, the clothes and shoes you're wearing—are made of plant and animal fossils (better known as oil and gas). If your walls and ceiling are built of plaster or plasterboard, they contain gypsum—and if they're painted, they're covered with calcite and maybe some mica, too.

Even the food you eat is packed with minerals. Common table salt is actually tiny crystals of halite, or sodium chloride, formed thousands of years ago from evaporating prehistoric seas.

See? Your house really is full of rocks and minerals. Now take a look outdoors. (By the way, that glass window you're looking through is made of quartz sand.) Your sidewalk is paved with concrete (a mixture of crushed

gravel, ground limestone, and sand). Most roads and streets are covered with asphalt (made from petroleum). Those cars driving by are running on gasoline extracted from fossils (oil). Automobiles, in fact, are a regular rock-and-mineral soup: glass from quartz, metal from ores, wire from copper, microprocessors from silicon chips, and plastic and fabric from petroleum. Why, the "rubber" tires alone contain zinc, sulfur, limestone, barite, magnesium, and a few different kinds of clays!

Above left: Mount Rushmore in South Dakota

Above: These skyscrapers are made almost entirely of rocks and minerals, from their cement foundation and marble walls, to their steel beams and glass windows. Charlotte, North Carolina

We use rocks and minerals in all sorts of ways: for building, for art, for tools, for medicine, for industry, for transportation. We make monuments of them to honor our heroes. We grind them into powder to make fertilizer and other chemicals. We wear them on our bodies, around our necks, and on our fingers. Why, rocks and minerals have been so important to humans for so long we even use them to describe our civilization's early history: The Stone Age, The Bronze Age, The Iron Age.

But whoa! Wait a minute! Earth's gifts to us, including its rocks and minerals, aren't endless. If we use them up, they'll be gone for good. Recycling the materials we've already used is a better idea than just digging up more.

Paperweight

When you become a rock collector, you will soon be faced with a problem: what to do with all the beautiful specimens you've found and just can't throw away. This paperweight is a good way to display small rocks because the water in it makes the colors and textures of the rocks look brighter and clearer.

What You Need

- *Clean, empty jar with a tight-fitting, screw-on lid*
- *Rocks, fossils, or seashells*
- *Enough water to fill the jar*
- *Chlorine laundry bleach*

What You Do

1. Remove the label from the jar by soaking the jar in warm water for 15 minutes.

2. Wash the rocks, fossils, or shells and place them in the jar.

3. Add water until the jar is three-quarters full. Then add bleach to completely fill the jar. (The bleach will keep algae from growing in the jar.)

4. Screw the lid on tightly. Wipe any water from the outside of the jar and the lid.

5. Turn the jar upside down to be sure it doesn't leak. If it does leak, try tightening the lid. If it still leaks, you may need to use a different jar and lid.

Sand CLOCK

Centuries ago, before mechanical clocks were developed, sand was used to measure time. You can build a sand clock of your own to time all kinds of things— how long you want to stay on the telephone, how long to cook an egg, or how much time you want to spend cleaning your room!

What You Need

- *2 identical clear plastic bottles with screw-on tops, such as small bottled-water containers*
- *1 cup (96 g) of dry sand*
- *Sifter*
- *Bowl*
- *Funnel or piece of stiff paper rolled into a funnel*
- *Cork that fits snugly into the top of the bottles; use an old cork or buy one at a hardware store*
- *Plastic drinking straw*
- *Ruler*
- *Sharp knife*
- *⅛-inch (.5 cm) drill bit*
- *Hand drill or a brace and bit*
- *Clock or watch with a second hand*
- *Acrylic paints*
- *Paintbrush*

WHAT YOU DO

1. Wash the bottles and remove the labels. Remove and throw away the screw-on lids.

2. Sift the cup (96 g) of sand into the bowl. Be sure to get out all sticks, pebbles, and other debris. Also be sure the sand is completely dry. If it is damp, spread it out on a baking sheet for a day or so until it is dry.

3. Use the funnel (or the rolled piece of stiff paper) to help pour the clean sand into one of the bottles.

4. **Ask an adult to help you cut the end off the cork** so that it's about 1 inch (2.54 cm) long.

5. **Ask an adult to help you drill a hole down the center of the cork,** clear through to the other side. After you have drilled the hole, push the drill bit in and out of it a few times to clean out all crumbs of cork. This hole must be clean and smooth so that sand flows through it without sticking. To make it perfectly smooth, press a segment of the plastic drinking straw inside the hole as a liner. **1**

6. Plug the cork into the neck of the bottle that has the sand in it. Let half the cork stay sticking out. Now press the other bottle onto the cork, so that the two bottles are held together by the cork. **2**

7. The next step takes some patience. You must time the sand clock and adjust it so that it takes the right amount of time for the sand to drop from one bottle to the other. Turn the sand clock so that the bottle with the sand in it is on the top. Use your watch or clock to time how long it takes for all of the sand to drop down to the bottom bottle. If the sand stops flowing, carefully unplug the top bottle, and clean out the cork hole. Be sure to take out whatever was clogging up the hole. Then pour all the sand back into one bottle and start timing again from the beginning. It may take several tries before the sand flows smoothly. Once you know how long it takes the sand to travel from one bottle to the other, either add sand or take away sand to get the right amount for the time you want. For example, if you want your clock to be a five-minute clock, add or take away sand until it takes exactly five minutes for the sand in the top bottle to fall to the bottom bottle.

8. Decorate your sand clock with acrylic paints and enjoy watching the passing of time.

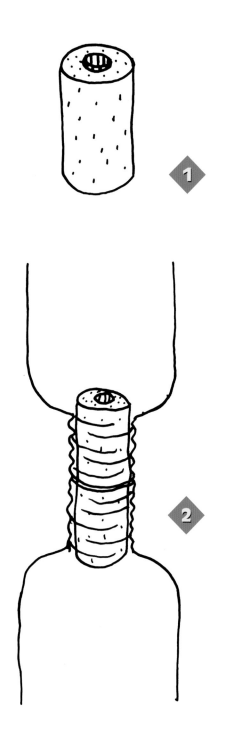

Trivet

Here's something useful and pretty to make when your collection of pebbles and rocks gets out of control! Use this trivet under hot dishes when you bring them to the table. You could also use it under a potted plant to catch drips of water.

What You Need

- *Sandpaper*
- *Piece of wood, about 6 by 6 inches (15 by 15 cm)*
- *Acrylic paint—any color that looks good with your pebbles*
- *2 paintbrushes, one thin, one fat*
- *Collection of pebbles of different colors, textures, and shapes: You can buy pebbles in pet stores that sell aquarium supplies if you don't have a collection of pebbles or can't find any you like.*
- *Waterproof craft glue*

What You Do

1. First sand the edges of the wood so they are smooth. Then use the thin paintbrush to paint one side and all four edges with acrylic paint.

2. While the paint is drying, plan your design. Move the pebbles around on a tabletop until you like the way they look. You might draw a sketch of your design to help yourself remember where to glue the pebbles.

3. When the paint is completely dry, use the fat paintbrush to spread a thick layer of glue in the first part of the design that you want to work on. Press the pebbles into the glue, making sure they are pressed against the board and surrounded by glue. The glue will dry clear, so don't worry about any glue globs!

4. Continue spreading glue and adding pebbles until the wood is completely covered. Fill in any open places or gaps between pebbles. Let the trivet dry overnight. It may take more than one day for the glue to dry depending on the weather. You can tell the glue is dry if it is clear.

Rocks for Building

Suppose you're an architect and your boss, the Pharaoh of all Egypt, wants you to build him something special, something big and impressive—and something that won't need painting or a new roof every few years. You suggest—a palm leaf and log pyramid? Off to the slave galleys, nincompoop! (Oh, now you say a stone pyramid...)

Rock buildings and steps on the volcanic island of Santorini, Greece.

The pyramids in Giza, Egypt.

For thousands of years, stone has been the natural choice for building. That's why the Egyptian pyramids and most other famous buildings and monuments from the past are still standing. Rock is tough, although, over millions of years, weather and other natural forces can wear down rock (see "Weather Wear," page 70).

The great pyramids of Egypt were built mostly of limestone taken from a quarry near Cairo. The largest of the pyramids, the Great Pyramid of King Khufu, has more than two million cut blocks of limestone, each weighing between two and four tons (1.8 and 3.6 t)! Most limestones used for building contain the fossils of shells from ancient seas. Because it's plentiful, limestone is the main ingredient in many famous structures, including the Notre Dame Cathedral in Paris.

Sandstone is another kind of sedimentary building rock used all over the world. Some types are too crumbly, but others are hard as, umm, rock. Different kinds are different colors, ranging from light to dark. Have you ever heard of New York City's famous "brownstone" houses and apartment buildings? They're made of brown sandstone. In Delhi, India, the spectacular impe-

rial palace called Red Fort is made of (you guessed it!) red sandstone. And the White House, in Washington, DC, is built of—well, actually, it's light-colored Virginia sandstone, painted white.

The fanciest of building rocks, marble, is limestone that has changed under pressure, becoming metamorphic. Pure marble is white, but other kinds of marbles have minerals in them that add color all over or in streaks or veins or swirls. Because of their handsome colors and smooth shiny surface, marbles give buildings an elegant look. One of the world's most impressive buildings, the Taj Mahal, is built of polished white marble decorated with inlaid gems!

Granite is harder than limestone, sandstone, or marble, so it stands up to weather best—but it's also the most difficult to cut into blocks. There are white, pink, red, gray, and black granites. Because it can be polished like marble but lasts longer, granite is a favorite for monuments and skyscrapers. The Greeks and Romans built many of their temples from granite. The Empire State Building is mostly granite.

These days, buildings are constructed mainly of man-made stone such as brick and concrete. But those materials begin with natural rock, too. Brick is made from soft clay that has been baked and hardened in a kiln. Concrete is a mixture of ground limestone, sand, gravel, and water. It was invented by the Romans, who used it to build such famous landmarks as the Colosseum in Rome, Italy.

MODEL Earth HOUSE

The earth is the most plentiful of all building materials. Many Native Americans living in the southwestern United States build adobe houses—houses made of mud and straw bricks. In this project you will make your own miniature adobe bricks and then use them to build model houses. The adults in your home will probably want to help with this project, because everyone likes to play in the mud. (Tell them to get their own bucket of clay!)

WHAT YOU NEED

- Bucket
- Trowel
- Bucket of soil that is mostly clay
- Old newspapers
- Water
- Strainer made of coarse wire screen or a garden sifter

- Sturdy wooden spoon or stick
- Plastic dishpan
- Trowel of sand
- Scissors
- Handful of dried grass or straw
- Piece of cardboard about 2 by 3 feet (61 by 91 cm)
- Aluminum foil

- *Piece of wood approximately 1 inch (2.54 cm) thick, 2 inches (5 cm) wide, and 1 to 2 feet (31 to 61 cm) long; an old wooden ruler will do*
- *Metal spatula or dull dinner knife*
- *10 to 12 sticks as wide and long as pencils*
- *20 to 22 round sticks, slightly thinner than pencils, and about 10 inches (25 cm) long*
- *Several flat wooden sticks, such as frozen dessert sticks or wooden coffee stirrers*
- *Piece of black construction paper*

WHAT YOU DO

1. Adobe bricks are made of clay, sand, straw, and water. When dried in the sun, they become hard. To make your miniature bricks, you need to find soil that has a lot of clay in it. (See "Hunting for Clay" on page 77).

2. Once you have your bucket of this kind of soil, you have to clean all big pebbles and other debris out of it. First, dump half the soil onto a pile of newspapers. Then, add water to the soil in the bucket and stir until the soil is completely mixed with the water. Next, pour the watery soil through the strainer into the dishpan. Throw away the pebbles and debris, and repeat the process until you have strained all of your soil. You now have a dishpan full of watery clay. Let it sit for a while until the soil settles to the bottom and you can scoop off most of the water.

3. Add a trowel of sand to the wet soil and stir until it is well mixed.

4. Use the scissors to cut the dry grass into tiny pieces, no longer than ¼ inch (1 cm)—the smaller, the better. Since your bricks will be small, the straw needs to be much smaller than real straw, too.

5. Add the straw to the brick mix and stir it well.

6. Cover the cardboard with aluminum foil. The foil will keep the bricks from sticking to the cardboard while they are drying.

7. Use the trowel to scoop out the wet mix onto the foil-covered cardboard. Drain off as much water as you can while lifting it out of the dishpan. Make a big flat cake, about ½ inch (1.5 cm) thick.

8. Put the cardboard in a sunny spot and let the clay and straw cake dry for about an hour.

9. After an hour, the cake should be partly dry. You will now cut it into bricks. First, use the flat stick to square up the edges of the big cake. Then use the spatula or knife to slice the cake into long strips, each about 1 inch (2.5 cm) wide.

may be too big. If the bricks crumble, mix up another batch but use less sand and smaller pieces of dried grass.

12. Now for the fun part. Peel the aluminum foil off the cardboard so you can use the cardboard as a base for your adobe house. Use some leftover adobe mud mixed with water for mortar to glue the bricks together. Here are some things to remember in building an adobe house:

～ *Lay the first row of bricks end to end, as in figure* **1**. *Lay the next row so that the bricks cover the cracks between the bricks on the first row.* **2**

～ *Put mortar on the bottom of each brick before you lay it in place. Simply hold the brick and press it into a puddle of wet mortar.*

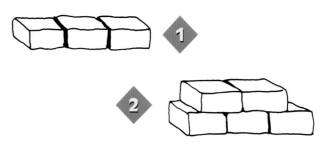

～ *For windows and doorways, lay a flat stick across the top of the opening (this is called a* lintel*), and then lay bricks on top of the lintel.* **3**

10. Now slice each long strip into ½ inch (1.5 cm) wide bricks. As you slice the bricks, use the knife to gently nudge the brick away from its neighbors so that all of its sides are open and it can dry better.

11. Place the cardboard full of bricks in a sunny spot to finish drying. This can take anywhere from another hour to another day, depending on the wetness of the mud and on the weather. When the bricks are dry, they will be hard and you can easily pick them up and handle them. If they are crumbly, they may have too much sand in them or the straw pieces

*When you get to the top of the house, lay a row of peeled pencil-sized sticks across the walls, as in figure **4**. These sticks are called* vegas, *and they are made of peeled pine logs in real adobe houses. Place bricks between the vegas.* **5**

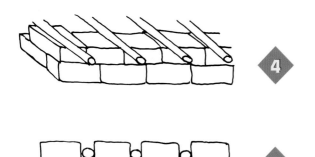

On top of the vegas, lay a roof of the thinner sticks. In a real adobe house, roofing paper would be placed over these sticks, so cut some black paper to the right size and place it on top to make the roof. Put a little mortar on top of some of the roof sticks to help hold the paper in place.

You can add a room or rooms to your house by building walls out from the first set of walls and laying vegas from wall to wall. **6**

Adobe houses usually have thick walls and not many windows. They are warm in winter and cool in summer because their thick walls provide good insulation. These houses are best suited to dry climates, because rain is their natural enemy. If heavy rains begin to wash away the walls, people can add more adobe mud to the walls to make them strong again.

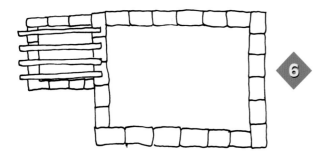

WINDOW Garden

SOME PLANTS STORE ENERGY AND FOOD IN ENLARGED ROOTS, SUCH AS BULBS AND TUBERS. YOU CAN GROW THESE PLANTS WITHOUT SOIL AS LONG AS YOU PROVIDE WATER AND A ROCKY BED FOR THEM. THIS IS A GOOD PROJECT TO SHOW OFF BEAUTIFUL COLORED OR UNUSUAL ROCKS THAT YOU FIND.

WHAT YOU NEED

- *Flower bulbs or carrots, radishes, turnips, or any other tuberous vegetable*
- *A collection of small- to medium-size pretty rocks*
- *A shallow bowl or an old pie tin*
- *Water*

WHAT YOU DO

1. If you are growing flower bulbs, you will first have to give the bulbs a cold period by putting them in a paper bag in the refrigerator for a few weeks. It is necessary to do this because bulbs naturally go through a cold winter outdoors before they sprout in spring. Making them sprout on a different schedule than their natural one is called *forcing bulbs*. Some garden centers sell precooled bulbs for forcing. They usually sell paper-white narcissus during late autumn. If you can't find these, or if you want to force tulip or other bulbs at a different time of year, simply give them a cool period in your own refrigerator.

2. Wash the rocks, then arrange them in the bowl or pie tin in a single layer.

3. If you are growing vegetables, trim off the bottom ½ inch (1.2 cm) or so of the fat part of the vegetable to give it a flat base to sit on.

4. Arrange the cooled bulbs or the trimmed vegetables on top of the rocks. If you are forcing bulbs, prop up the bulbs with rocks, but do not completely cover them. Be sure to plant the bulbs right side up.

5. Pour in enough water to wet the bottoms of the bulbs or vegetables.

6. Place your rock garden in a sunny window. Check it every day, and add water as needed. In a few days you should begin to see sprouts. Bulbs will take several weeks to bloom, but keep adding water, and your patience will be rewarded when you have beautiful flowers blooming in your house in the middle of winter!

TIN Lantern

Long ago people made lanterns out of tin. The tin protected the candle from drafts while the holes punched in the tin let light out in a pretty pattern. This lantern is simple to make and, when the candle inside is lit, will cast beautiful dancing light on the walls and ceiling of a darkened room.

WHAT YOU NEED

- Empty aluminum can
- Black marker
- Sturdy log, nearly as wide as the can
- 2 or 3 nails of different widths
- Hammer
- Can opener—the type used to make triangular punctures
- Paintbrush
- Acrylic paints
- Small candle
- Candle holder

What You Do

1. Thoroughly clean the can and dry it.

2. Lightly mark the outside of the can with dots where you want to create your pattern with holes. Your design should appear all around the can and on the unopened side.

3. Lay the can on the floor and slip the log inside it until the wood touches the unopened end. Use one of your legs to hold the log securely against the floor.

4. Use the hammer and nails to make holes through the can where you have made marks. Ask a friend or adult to hold the can still while you hammer.

5. Remove the log. Use the can opener to make large holes on the unopened end of the can (this will be the top of the lantern).

6. Paint a design all over the outside of the can.

7. Place the candle in the candle holder and put it on a table or mantle. **Ask an adult to light the candle.** Make sure the candle is at least 2 inches (5 cm) shorter than the height of the lantern. Place the can over the lit candle, turn out the lights, and enjoy the show!

Metals from Minerals

Imagine you're a cave person thousands of years ago and you've just found a pretty blue or green rock. You figure you'll pound the rock into powder, mix in some grease, and make paint for decorating the cave walls. But sheesh, no matter how hard you hammer on it, the pesky rock won't break. Instead, it bends and flattens. What a worthless hunk of—hey, wait a minute. Maybe you could pound the stuff into the shape of a knife blade or scraper. That would be a lot easier than chipping away at flint. Hmmm....

Of course, nobody knows for sure, but that could be how the Stone Age ended and the Copper Age began. Scientists do know that humans began making tools of copper instead of stone about 10,000 years ago. A few thousand years later, someone discovered that you could make an even stronger metal by mixing a little *tin* with the copper. That mixture, the first *alloy*, was *bronze*. Bronze made sharper swords that could cut through a copper shield. Goodbye Copper Age, hello Bronze Age.

Eventually, about 4,000 years ago, ancient metalworkers learned to mine rock that contained iron, a super-strong and easy-to-sharpen metal. They heated

Copper

Pyrite

the ore in fire until the iron melted away from the rock, then hammered it into the shape of tools and weapons. That was the beginning of The Iron Age.

Many minerals, such as pyrite, magnetite, and marcasite, cointain small amounts of metals.

Minerals with large amounts of metals that can easily be separated are called *ore minerals*. These rocks are mined from the Earth's crust or dredged from lakes or streams. Then the ore is crushed and the metal is extracted from the "waste" rock and heated, or smelted, to make pure metal, like the eight major types described below.

Aluminum is the third most common element in Earth's crust and the most common metal. Aluminum is hard to take out of most rocks, except for the one called bauxite. Bauxite ore gives us strong, lightweight aluminum for buildings, cars and planes, foil, pots and pans, and lots of other uses.

Copper is the great-great-granddaddy of all metals. Workers used copper chisels to cut stone blocks for the pyramids! Today we still use copper for such things as wire and water pipes. We also mix copper with *zinc* to

Azurite / Malachite

make the alloy *brass*, and with tin to make bronze. Copper ores are colorful and look great in a collection. Some of the most important are chalcopyrite (gold-colored), *azurite* (blue), and *malachite* (green).

Iron is a really important metal. It's tough and hard but melts easily, so it can be poured into molds or flattened into sheets. We mix it with carbon and other elements to make alloys such as cast iron, wrought iron, and the most-used metal in the world: steel. *Hematite*, a bubbly

Magnesite

looking mineral, is the main iron ore.

Lead is made from *galena*, a black, shiny mineral that's often found in limestone or with silver. Galena crystals are perfectly square and are used in crystal radio sets. Lead is used mostly in batteries and in materials that protect us against X rays and radioactivity.

Nickel is a strong, tough metal that stands up to high temperatures and hard wear. It's used mainly to add strength to alloys such as steel. It's also mixed with copper to make coins. The American nickel, or five-cent piece, has three times as much copper as nickel! The main nickel ores are *pyrrhotite* and *pentlandite*. Most meteorites contain nickel, too!

Tin comes from a hard, heavy ore called *cassiterite*. Tin is used mostly for plating metal products such as cans. It's also mixed with copper to make bronze, and with lead to make *pewter*.

Zinc is produced from an ore called *sphalerite*. The rock is usually dark black but can also be red, yellow, or green, so it's tricky to identify. Zinc is used to make brass and to give metals a protective coating.

Mercury is the only metal that's liquid even when it's not hot. It comes from an earthy red ore called cinnabar that is found in only a few places in the world, such as Spain, Italy, and the western United States. Mercury is used in thermometers, barometers, and as an ingredient in medicines and paint pigments.

Marcasite

Gold, Silver, and Platinum

Have you ever dreamed of finding a treasure chest? Eagerly, you open the lid and peer inside. It's full to the brim with pieces of—hey, what's this? Iron?

Not many people would jump for joy at finding a chest of iron or nickel or any of the other ordinary metals. But a box of gold! Wow!

For centuries we humans have valued *gold* and *silver* above all other metals. Over the past 100 years *platinum* has become an important precious metal, too. What makes them so special?

Platinum, gold, and silver aren't the rarest metals on earth. But they are uncommon—and, even more important—they're uncommonly beautiful. They glitter and shine. They're soft and easy to shape. And they don't rust or lose their beauty over the years.

Gold is especially good at keeping its spectacular appearance. When divers find gold coins from ancient shipwrecks, the coins are as bright and shiny as the day they were made—even after being buried in mud and sand and salt water for hundreds of years!

Silver is less valuable than gold partly because its surface reacts with the air around it and gradually darkens or tarnishes. Silver has to be polished occasionally to remove the tarnish and bring back its bright shine.

Platinum doesn't tarnish but also doesn't have the glamorous gleam of its cousins. Platinum is actually more valuable than gold, though, because it's in great demand in industry, for oil refining and for making low-pollution car exhaust systems.

It's no wonder that gold, silver, and platinum are prized for making jewelry, tableware, and other objects. All three are amazingly *ductile* (DUCK-tuhl). That means they can be hammered flat, stretched into wire, or molded into almost any imaginable shape. In 1902, a silversmith made a pair of silver water jugs for the Maharajah of Jaipur, India that are five feet three inches (160 cm) tall and hold 2,160 gallons (8,176 l) each!

Gold is the most workable of all the precious metals. It can be hammered into sheets, called gold leaf, so flat and thin that a stack of 250,000 is only one inch (2.5 cm) high! An ounce (or 28 grams) of gold can be heated and stretched to make a wire 60 miles (96 km) long! Egypt's famous King Tutanhkamun was buried in a coffin made of more than a ton of solid gold. China's emperors once wore robes woven of gold thread.

Of course, for centuries countries also have been using gold and silver for making coins. Platinum has been used for coins, too. Back in the days of Czar Nicholas I, Russian three-ruble pieces were platinum.

But precious metals are used for more than just money and luxuries. Over a third of all the silver mined in the United States is used for making and developing photographic film. Dentists use gold, silver, and platinum for fillings. And because they're terrific conductors of electricity, the metals also are used in electrical components, circuit boards, and computer chips.

Gold

Platinum, silver, and gold are called *native* metals because they can be found in nature as pure metal. They don't always have to be processed into metal from mineral ore, the way aluminum has to be made from bauxite or lead from galena. Silver is mined either way; as "free" silver in *veins* or clumps, or in ores such as *argentite*. Most platinum occurs as small grains or flakes of free metal in nickel deposits. Gold is usually found in veins among quartz or with deposits of *pyrite*, a duller, brassy-looking mineral that's also called "fools' gold" because over-eager miners often mistake it for the real thing.

Chapter 5

Collecting Rocks and Minerals

Have you ever picked up a really pretty or interesting rock and brought it home? Do you have a special box where you keep favorite rocks and other neat stuff? Then you've already started a collection!

Collecting rocks and minerals is a lot of fun. You can do it almost all the time, anytime: when you're walking with your friends, when you travel to different places, when you're exploring your neighborhood. After all, rocks are everywhere. You'll never run out of things to collect!

At first, you'll probably want to keep all sorts of rocks—anything that's especially beautiful or shiny or smooth or sparkly or bumpy or crumbly or…well, you get the idea. That's how most great collections start.

Sooner or later, though, you'll probably decide to specialize. Some people try to collect just one of as many different kinds of rocks and minerals as they can find. Others collect just certain types, such as igneous or metamorphic, or just rocks from certain places. You can build all sorts of different special collections: crystals, rocks from your home state or county, gemstones, rocks from your backyard; rocks from stream beds, fossils, rocks from the seashore, rocks you found on your summer vacation, rocks and minerals from foreign countries. The possibilities are endless!

Naturally, you'll want to show off your favorite specimens. You can build a collection box like the one on page 143, or you can buy plastic boxes with separate compartments.

Here are some other tips to help you build a terrific collection.

■ Don't worry if you can't figure out what kind of rocks or minerals you have. The pictures in field guides and geology books don't always look exactly like the specimens you find. Even professional geologists sometimes have a hard time identifying! Instead, label the rocks in your collection according to where you found them. Then, if you think you know what kind a specimen is, you can add that too.

■ Try not to gather too many rocks when you go collecting! Remember, rocks are a part of nature. Pick a few good specimens for your collection and leave the rest where you find them, undisturbed.

■ One of the best ways to learn more about collecting rocks and minerals is to join a rock hound club. Chances are there's one in your area. You'll learn the best places to go to look for specimens, and you might even be able to trade rocks with other members.

■ Look at other rock and mineral collections in museums, the geology department of a local college, and rock shops. Rock shops are an especially good place to buy hard-to-find specimens. Most also sell "starter" sets of mounted minerals for beginners.

■ Read books about geology and collecting rocks and minerals. Also, look in your local library or bookstore for collecting-site guides: books that describe and give directions to the best places in your region for finding good specimens.

Sand
PAINTING

For hundreds of years, people from many cultures have created sand paintings as part of important ceremonies. Other sand paintings are not meant to last: they are made on the ground, and when the ceremony is over, the wind blows the art away. The sand painting in this project is one that you can keep. Designs made with colored sand have beautiful texture, as well as color.

WHAT YOU NEED

- *Coarse sifter or a piece of coarse window screen cloth*
- *Bucket of sand: If you want to use natural-colored sand and can find different shades of sand, collect a small container of each color; if you will need to add color to the sand, collect or buy a bucket of clean sand.*
- *Containers for each color of sand that you will use; paper cups or small plastic containers work well*
- *Powdered tempera paints; sold at craft-supply stores. If you can't find powdered tempera, liquid ones will work, but you will have to let the sand dry before you paint with it.*
- *Spoon*
- *Pencil*
- *Scissors*
- *Cardboard, cut to the size you want your finished painting to be*
- *White craft glue in a squeeze bottle*
- *Soft paintbrush*
- *Container of water*

WHAT YOU DO

1. Begin by sifting the sand to get rid of any pebbles, sticks, or pieces of leaves.

2. Now you are ready to color the sand. If you are using natural- colored sands, skip this step. To color sand, mix a spoonful of powdered tempera paint

into 1 cup (200 g) of sand. Stir until the sand is evenly colored. If you are using liquid tempera, stir the paint and sand until the sand is evenly colored. Then spread the sand out in a pie pan for a few hours so that it can dry before you use it.

3. Lightly draw your design onto the piece of cardboard. Plan where each color of sand will be.

4. Squeeze glue into the area where the first color will be.

5. Use the spoon to help pour sand onto the glue covered area. Completely cover the area with a thick layer of sand.

6. Wait a few minutes until the glue is almost dry, then gently tap the leftover, loose sand back into its container. When you do this, particles of sand will probably get in places where you don't want them. Don't worry; as long as these sand grains are not sitting on top of wet glue, you will be able to brush them off after everything has dried.

7. Brush any stray sand off the cardboard with the dry paintbrush, and put glue on the next area that you want to paint. Repeat steps 5 and 6 until the painting is finished.

8. If you want to add any colors on top of areas that are already painted, squeeze glue only where you want the added color to be, and pour sand onto the wet glue, just as you did with the first coatings of sand. You can continue to build up layers, but let the glue dry in between layers.

9. Let the entire painting dry overnight.

10. When the painting is dry, use the dry brush to gently brush colored sand off areas where it shouldn't be. If any sand sticks to the top of other colors, simply add a little bit of glue on top of these grains, and sprinkle on a thin layer of the right color sand; let that dry, too.

11. If the colors of your sand painting look dull, paint over each colored area with water. Clean the brush before moving to a different color.

Gearing Up

You don't need a lot of fancy equipment to collect rocks and minerals. You do need a few basic items, though, to make your hobby safer and to help you bring home top-notch specimens.

- **Geologist's hammer.** Use the square end for breaking collection-size pieces from large rocks. The pointed or chisel-shaped end is for prying or splitting rocks and for chipping away small chunks. Don't try to use an ordinary carpenter's hammer: the hammer will break instead of the rocks!

- **Safety glasses or plastic goggles.** Think of these as a part of your hammer and put them on every time you use that tool! They'll keep your eyes safe from sharp, flying bits of chipped rock. A good rock hound never forgets eye protection!

- **Cold steel chisels.** These are made from extra-hard steel and are handy when you need to carefully chip out a specimen from the surrounding rock. Get a ¼-inch (1 cm) chisel for small work and a ¾-inch or 1-inch (2 or 2.5 cm) chisel for bigger jobs.

- **Small backpack.** This is for carrying your equipment and the rocks and minerals you find. Look for a sturdy cloth pack with padded shoulder straps and at least one pocket for holding small items. Don't get a big pack or you'll be tempted to keep more rocks than you can comfortably carry! For a pack you can make yourself from an old pair of jeans, check out page 140.

- **Protective clothing.** Think about where you're going and the kind of rock hunting you'll be doing. If you're picking pebbles or small stones from a streambed, you don't need much protection. But if you'll be hammering or handling large chunks of rock, you should wear boots, gloves, sturdy cloth pants, and a long-sleeved shirt. It's a good idea to wear a safety helmet, too. Just in case it rains, pack something to keep you dry.

- **Hand lens or magnifying glass.** You'll need it for taking a close look at small crystals and fossils. Get one that folds into itself or has a case to protect the lens from accidental scratches.

- **Newspaper or small bags.** Wrap each rock and mineral you find in its own sheet of newspaper or put it in a sandwich-size paper or plastic bag. You might also want to bring along some tissue paper or empty plastic pill bottles for delicate finds such as small crystals.

- **Labels, a notebook, and pen or pencil.** You can buy small sticky-backed labels or use pieces of adhesive tape. For each specimen you bring home, put a number

Picture jasper

on a label and stick the label on the rock before you wrap it. Then write the same number in your notebook, and next to it jot down where you found the specimen, the date, and any other information you think is important. A typical notebook entry might read: "No. 14— Fossil found in limestone boulder near south end of Flat Rock Creek. June 10." Don't skip this step! You won't always remember when and where you found each and every specimen. For a notebook you can make yourself, see page 8.

- **Map and compass.** Always know exactly where you're going, how to get there, and how to get back!

- **First-Aid Supplies.** For cuts and scratches, bring a supply of adhesive bandages and a tube of antibiotic ointment. On long field trips, carry a complete Red Cross–approved first-aid kit.

- **Specimen Cleaning Tools.** Keep these at home for cleaning the rocks and minerals you find. Use a toothbrush or paintbrush to remove loose dirt and dust. A nail file or small knife works great for cleaning off hardened clay or mud. A dentist's pick or a large needle is handy for working with delicate fossils or crystals. Of course, you can wash most specimens with water—but be careful. Some minerals dissolve in water! If you're not sure about a specimen, soak a small piece in water for several hours to see if it shrinks or disappears.

Finding Rocks and Minerals

Where's the best place to look for rocks and minerals? Just look down! You can find at least a few rocks to examine almost anywhere. On the other hand, if you're hoping to discover some really great specimens, ones that are special enough to keep for your collection, you might need to look a little harder.

Rocks collect in places where the water slows down: behind boulders or other obstacles in the stream, for instance, and around sharp bends.

Ocean beaches can be good places to find pebble-size specimens. In places such as the Coastal Northwest in the United States, beachcombing rock hounds can pick up gemstones such as *onyx*, *agate*, and *jasper*, already smoothed and polished by the ocean waves! The best time to look is at low tide, especially just after a storm. The cliffs along rocky seashores also offer good places to search for specimens.

Lots of rock is exposed at quarries, where commercial types such as granite or marble or limestone are mined to be sold. Quarries can be excellent places for finding rocks, minerals, and fossils—but they also can be dangerous. **Be sure to get permission before entering a quarry, and never go without an adult.**

The best bets are places where nature, or humans, have already done some digging for you and have uncovered lots of rock. Cuts through hills or mountains where construction crews built highways or railroad beds are excellent prospecting sites. So are gullies, gulches, and ravines where rivers or streams have washed away the soil. Look carefully along the sides of these areas for rocks exposed by erosion. Other good places to look are natural outcrops, such as the stony faces of hills and mountains, where wind and rain have uncovered Earth's bedrock.

Streambeds can be great rock-hounding sites, too. Sometimes you'll find minerals that have tumbled along in the current for dozens or even hundreds of miles.

Of course, you won't find every kind of rock and mineral right in your own area. Different types of rocks and minerals come from different parts of the world. Try to include a few rock-hunting side trips when you travel or go on vacation.

Finally, there's one sort of rock-hunting site that's absolutely guaranteed to have great specimens: a rock shop! Finding your own rocks and minerals in the field is fun, but most rock hounds also buy specimens to add to their collections. Rock shops are great places to get a good look at many different kinds of rocks and minerals. The owners often are able to give you directions to good collecting sites, too.

Backpack

It's handy to keep all your rock collecting equipment packed and ready to go. You can make this sturdy pack out of an old pair of blue jeans, even if you've never sewn anything in your life!

*Top to bottom:
Mica, turquoise,
red lace agate,
agate, turquoise*

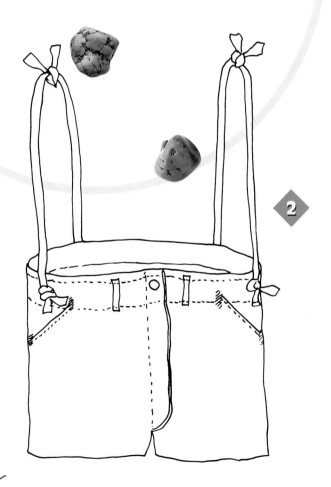

1

2

What You Need

- *Old pair of blue jeans*
- *Scissors*
- *Sewing needle*
- *Heavy thread, such as button thread*

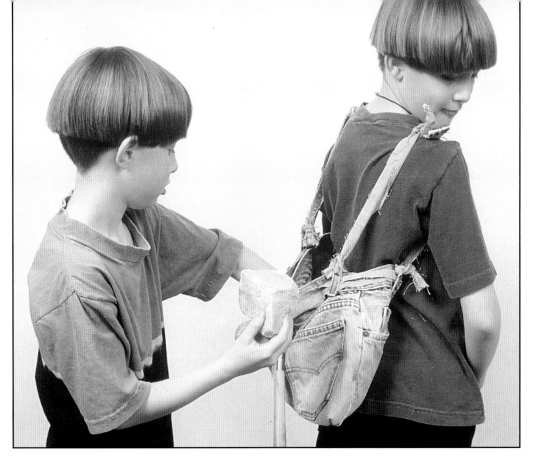

WHAT YOU DO

1. Cut off both legs of the jeans. Cut about 2 inches (5 cm) below the top of each leg.

2. Turn the jeans inside out.

3. Thread the needle with about 36 inches (91 cm) of thread. Tie a big knot in the end of the thread.

4. Make a running stitch going across each leg opening. To make a running stitch, poke the needle in near one edge. Pull the needle through the cloth, and stick it in again about ¼ inch (1 cm) away from the place where it came out of the first stitch. **1**

5. Repeat this step all the way across the leg. Tie a knot by poking the tip of the needle through a loop in the thread. Then cut the thread close to the knot.

6. After you have sewn both seams, trim the cloth about ½ inch (1.5 cm) away from the seams.

7. Turn the jeans right side out again. Now the seams will be on the inside and you won't be able to see them.

8. To make straps from the leg pieces of the jeans, cut a long strip from each leg seam, about 1 inch (2.5 cm) wide. You will have four long strips with a seam down the middle of each. The seams will make the pieces of cloth extra strong.

9. Tie one long strip of cloth to each of the four belt loops in the front and back of the jeans. Now tie each pair of strips together. **2** You can slip the straps over your shoulders to use the pack as a backpack, or carry it by the straps over one shoulder.

10. Cut one more long strip from the leg part of the jeans. Thread this strip through the belt loops like a belt. You can use this to tie the pack closed to keep things from falling out.

11. Use the pockets to store the gear listed in "Gearing Up" on page 138. Hang a small hammer from one of the belt loops. When you're ready to hit the trail, add a water bottle and a snack. (Be sure to leave plenty of room in the pack for all your rocks!)

Safety Tips to Remember

Thousands of kids and adults spend their spare time looking for and collecting rocks and minerals. It's a terrific hobby that takes you outdoors to all sorts of interesting places. Finding a beautiful crystal or a really good fossil or rock specimen is exciting! But you have to be careful. Working around rocks and using hammers and other tools can be tricky.

Always remember that the most important safety rule in everything you do is: Think before you act. Use your head and your own good common sense. If you're about to do something or go somewhere that you know deep down might not be safe, stop. Just don't do it!

Here are some more suggestions for keeping your hobby safe and fun.

■ Always get permission before going on private property. Tell the landowner what you want to do and where you want to go. If you ask nicely and mention that you'll be careful not to leave gates open or hurt anything, you'll probably get an okay. This is important. Entering private property without permission is against the law. Also, the landowner may be able to warn you about any dangerous places on the property.

■ Don't go on a field trip alone. It's always safer to have at least one friend along, just in case you need help. Besides, it's more fun.

■ Plan ahead. Be sure an adult knows where you intend to go and when you will be back. Better yet, have an adult go with you.

■ Wear protective clothing. Safety goggles are a must. (See "Gearing Up" on page 138 for a complete list.)

■ Pack food and fresh water. Rock collecting is fun, but it's also strenuous. You'll work up a big appetite and thirst. Don't drink from streams, lakes, or ponds, though. Bring your own water.

Children safely supervised by an experienced adult, Mammoth Cave National Park, Mammoth, Kentucky

■ Stay away from quarries and mines unless you're with an experienced adult and have the property owner's permission. These are dangerous places. Shaky rock walls, heavy equipment, and hard-to-see cliffs and pits are only some of the hazards. Also, never go in a cave or underground mine without the supervision of an experienced adult.

■ Don't work directly beneath a low, steep rock wall. Loose rocks can fall from above without warning.

■ Bring a first-aid kit (see page 138). Also, it's a good idea to take a first-aid course. Local Scouting organizations and Red Cross chapters offer courses for kids and adults. Knowing first aid means knowing how to help if someone is injured!

ROCK
ollection
BOX

𝒜 COLLECTION BOX LETS YOU
DISPLAY YOUR BEST ROCK SPECI-
MENS AND PROTECTS THEM FROM
BEING THROWN OUTSIDE BY SOME-
ONE WHO THINKS THEY'RE JUST
ORDINARY ROCKS. THIS BOX IS
EASY TO FIND, AND YOU CAN TURN
IT INTO A REAL TREASURE CHEST
WITH A LITTLE IMAGINATION.

WHAT YOU NEED

- *Empty paper egg carton—any size will do; if you
  have too many rocks in your collection for the size
  of your egg carton, make more than one*
- *Water-soluble paints, such as acrylics or craft
  paints; look for bright metallic or pearlescent paints
  at a craft-supply store—watercolors DON'T work*
- *Paintbrush*
- *Container for water*
- *Scissors*
- *Stick-on labels*
- *Pen or marker*

WHAT YOU DO

1. Paint the egg carton inside and out with your favorite
   colors.

2. After the paint has dried, cut the labels into ½-inch
   (1.5 cm) square pieces. Write the name of each of
   your rocks on a label. Press each label into the bottom of one of the egg compartments.

3. Arrange your rocks in their compartments. That's all
   there is to it!

THANKS to all the children and their parents who helped us with making and photographing of projects; Hadas Ravé, for the Rock Mobile; Dana Irwin for the Tin Lantern; The Silver Armadillo, for the loan of so many gorgeous rocks and minerals; NASA, Celia Gomez with Carlsbad Caverns, and Vickie Carson with Mammoth Cave National Park, for loaning us several fabulous photos.

A SPECIAL thanks to photo librarian extraordinaire Joe McGregor, with the U.S. Geologic Survey, for providing us with a gold mine of outstanding photos.

THE KIDS (and a few parents)

Anna-Maria Apostolopoulos, 69, 84-85, 107, and 126; Nathan Baumgarten, 69 and 126; Dave Cicale, 28, 72, and 88-89; Michael and Paul Elliston, 28 and 72; Katelynn Graeme, with her Dad, Bob Graeme, 32-33, and 38-39, 54, and 129; Promise Hill, 96 and 104; Emily Hutchinson, 17, with friend's mom, Josena Aiello McCaig, 20, and 59; Jonathan D. Jones, 69, 84-84, with his Dad, Derrick Jones, 108-109, and 126; Jennifer Krahl, 48-49 and 91; Jesse and Josh Krautwurst, 74-75, with their mom, Laurel Krautwurst, 99, and 141; Ciara Rain McCaig, 17 and 59; Amanda McGrayne, 24, 69, 84-85, and 126; Jessica Oswald, 38-39, 54, and 129; Austin Sconyers-Snow, 77-78, 79-81, and 83; French Sconyers-Snow, 76, with their Dad, Jerry Snow, 81, and 83; Jonavan and Javonda Walker, 111-112 and 136-137

J 551.078-AND   Geology crafts for kids   ✓

Anderson, Alan   **DATE DUE**

APR 3 0 1997	AUG 1 4 2001			
JUN 2 3 1997	APR 1 5 2002			
DEC 1 9 1997	NOV 1 2 2003			
MAR 3 1998	NOV 2 3 2004			
APR 1 3 1998	APR 1 6 2005			
SEP 3 0 1998	APR 3 0 2005	WITHDRAWN		
MAR 2 7 2000	MAY 1 7 2006			
SEP 5 2000	2 0 2007			
SEP 2 8 2000	JA 1 0 08			
NOV 2 8 2000	OCT 1 7 2007			
FEB 5 2001	MAY 1 1 2009			
APR 1 2 2001	DEC 1 6 2010			
MAY - 9 2001	FEB 2 2013			